Herbert J. Spiro is Associate Professor of Political Science at Amherst College. This book is the result of his one-year trip throughout Africa in 1959-60 on Guggenheim, Fulbright, and Social Science Research Fellowships. Among Professor Spiro's other published works are "New Constitutional Forms in Africa," appearing in *World Politics,* October 1960, and *Government by Constitution: The Political Systems of Democracy* (1959).

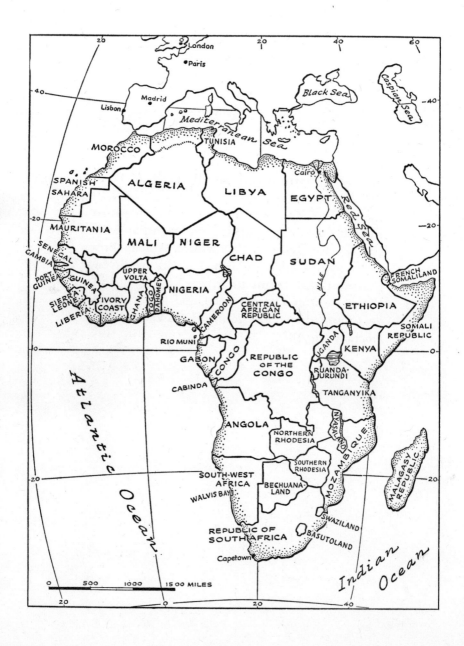

Herbert J. Spiro

Politics in Africa

Prospects South of the Sahara

Prentice-Hall, Inc., Englewood Cliffs, N.J.

1962

For

Peter John Spiro

© 1962 by Prentice-Hall, Inc., Englewood Cliffs, N.J.

Library of Congress Catalog Card No.: 62-9313

Printed in the United States of America

68522-C

Preface

To encourage a better understanding of politics in the new Africa, by looking at it with a new perspective, is the main aim of this book. The new perspective has been made necessary by the novelty of the political systems recently created in Africa south of the Sahara. This novelty consists of three major differences between older states and these new ones in Africa. In contrast to conventional sovereign nation-states, the new sub-Saharan members of the international community did not come into being, nor did their leaders come to the fore, through the use of organized force on a large scale. After achieving statehood, they have been less preoccupied with questions of territorial frontiers than their older models. None of the new states has a culturally homogeneous population and none intends to differentiate the culture of its people as much as possible from the cultures of its neighbors, as other nations have been culturally differentiated, deliberately, all over the globe. The new African states, therefore, lack the military, geographical, and cultural substance of the national states with which we are familiar. By recognizing this, they may be able to avoid many of the negative experiences—international and civil war, Irredentism, cultural chauvinism—through which most other states have passed, and are passing still, in the modern age. The new Africa may also make a positive contribution to the constitutional development of the global community of mankind.

We can recognize the novelty of African politics only by studying it with a new perspective that no longer looks upon Western constitutional democracy as the ultimate achievement of man's political genius. Our estimate of the prospects for Africa must not be based condescendingly upon the fidelity with which the new states copy political institutions and procedures which we happen to cherish. We must also take into account the human capacity to adapt and to innovate in the face of unprecedented problems. Neither party to the Cold War has shown that it possesses this capacity to a sufficient degree. Perhaps the Africans' freshness at modern politics will stimulate them into more imaginative creativity.

Throughout this book, I have tried to identify the most persistent

v

political patterns in the new states and the independence movements
that brought about their establishment. I have used the method
worked out in my *Government by Constitution: The Political Systems of Democracy.* I have had to rely heavily upon the writings of
contemporary students of African politics, and wish to acknowledge
my indebtedness especially to the pioneering studies of David E.
Apter, Gwendolen M. Carter, James S. Coleman, Thomas Hodgkin,
and O. Mannoni. A grant from the Rockefeller Foundation relieving
me from teaching duties in the fall term of 1958-59 enabled me to
prepare myself for my work in Africa. My research there in 1959-60
was made possible by grants from the John Simon Guggenheim
Foundation, the United States Education (Fulbright) Commission
in the United Kingdom, and Harvard University (by sabbatical
leave). I am grateful to all of these and also to the many people in
Africa, of different races, occupations, and political persuasions, who
offered my wife and myself their sincere hospitality, both domestic
and intellectual.

Some of the initiative for my African interest came from my
wife, Elizabeth Petersen Spiro, whose perceptions—often quite different from my own—may have improved my perspective. Both she
and Professor Rupert Emerson, from rather different points of view,
read and vigorously criticized the book in manuscript. I appreciate
their advice more than they may recognize in the finished product,
for which I gladly assume full responsibility.

Herbert J. Spiro

Amherst, Massachusetts
September 1961

Table of Contents

List of Maps

Chapter I

The New Africa in World Politics

*Seek ye first the political kingdom, and all other things shall
be added unto it.*

—Kwame Nkrumah

Africa's Leap onto the World Stage

The new states of Africa south of the Sahara crowded onto the
stage of world politics in 1960. Within a very few months, these African
countries and their African leaders forced upon the rest of the world
a new awareness of the existence of their continent and its problems.
They brought this new Africa-consciousness to both camps into which
the Cold War had divided the world, and especially to the Soviet
Union and the United States. Europeans had always been better informed about Africa and more interested in its affairs, because most
western European states had at one time or another been involved in
colonial ventures on the so-called Dark Continent. Most of these ventures, past or present, left Europeans with an only marginal concern
for Black Africa, until its eruption into world politics in the course of
1960.

Unlike western Europe, neither America nor Russia had had any
colonial experience in Africa. Soviet politicians and communist theo-
reticians had often used the activities of European states in Africa to
produce case studies in capitalist "colonialism" or "imperialism." But
they had been denied both access to the peoples south of the Sahara
and influence upon their development. One-tenth of the population of
the United States consisted of descendants of Africans brought here as
slaves. Despite this crude fact—perhaps because of it—American public
and official opinion had been generally ignorant of and disinterested

in the territories lying between the Sahara Desert to the north and the Limpopo River to the south. All this changed radically in 1960, when the new Africa executed its most dramatic leap onto the stage of world politics right inside the United States of America, at the "world historical theater" of the United Nations, in New York City.

American awareness of other great areas of the earth had been stimulated more gradually in earlier decades and centuries. The vast majority of Americans traced their descent from Europe, and Europe had always been at the back of the "American mind," sometimes in the attempt to emulate or surpass Europe, sometimes in the desire to isolate the United States from it. In the Far East, heavy commercial, missionary, and colonial commitments long preceded World War II, which, of course, for the United States started in the Pacific Ocean. After the war, new states truly "emerged" rather than erupted in East and South East Asia. American opinion and those who help to shape it, including the academic community, was relatively well prepared to understand these new members of the international community. This was also true of the Near East in the following years. Christian interest in the Holy Land and its neighbors had always been high in the United States, which had won one of its earliest naval victories against the Barbary Coast Pirates in North Africa, where, moreover, thousands of American troops had fought during World War II.

Africa south of the Sahara, "Black Africa," by contrast, had been left dark for most Americans through lack of any similar illumination. The slaves had come from there, and some freed slaves who returned founded Liberia. Its capital, Monrovia, was named after the same American President whose Monroe Doctrine was meant to keep new European colonial ventures out of the western hemisphere. Thousands of American missionaries tried to spread the Gospel in various parts of the Dark Continent. An occasional big game hunter like Teddy Roosevelt, and novelists like Ernest Hemingway, added to American lore about Africa. But most American awareness of Africa was in the realm of myth, until the second half of the 1950's.

The fact that a journalist with John Gunther's keen sensitivity to public needs then wrote his *Inside Africa*, which became a best seller, presaged the hunger for information about Africa, which has yet to be stilled. Some of this appetite grew by what it fed on during the next few years: more or less sensationalist fiction about the outrages of Mau Mau or the tragedies of race relations in South Africa. Such novels were usually written by Europeans or white Africans. Most of the knowledge that Americans gained about Africa during these years was collected, digested, and presented for them by Europeans. It was, therefore, bound to be flavored by the outlook and attitudes of the colonial powers or the white minorities resident in Africa. As a result, regardless of the honesty of these authors, the pictures they had painted for their American readers often led them to react in a very "European," and sometimes even "colonial," way to the torrent of African events reported to the American public in the year 1960.

On New Year's Day of 1960, Cameroon, which had been a United Nations Trusteeship Territory under French administration, celebrated its independence. Armed troops guarded the airport, where diplomats —including President Eisenhower's special ambassadors—arrived, against attacks threatened by the elected government's outlawed opposition. Before the year was over, violence had flared up in many sub-Saharan countries. So many new African states were admitted to the United Nations, that the Continent as a whole accounted for more than a fourth of the total membership of the world organization. At Sharpeville in the Union of South Africa, government police fired upon an African crowd, killing more than sixty Africans, with the result that the United States for the first time voted explicitly against South Africa in the United Nations. Belgium granted independence to its Congo, whose elected government subsequently requested the help of the United Nations in restoring order. The UN responded with its biggest international military operation since Korea, only to expose itself and its Secretary General to charges of colonialism. These accusations were made not only by the Soviet Premier, but apparently echoed by African leaders, including the Presidents of Ghana and Guinea, who openly consulted with Khrushchev in New York during the meeting of the United Nations General Assembly. On several votes, some African states sided with the Soviets against the West. In the course of the presidential election campaign of 1960, both Republican and Democratic speakers repeatedly referred to past or future African policies of the United States for partisan purposes. After his victory, the President-elect announced the appointment of his new Assistant Secretary of State for African Affairs before he selected his Secretary of State, and gave the position to a prominent Democratic politician who had been Governor of Michigan for six terms. During the campaign, John F. Kennedy had his picture taken with Tom Mboya, a politician from Kenya, who secured a promise for substantial grants of money for African scholarships to the United States from the Kennedy family foundation.

By the end of 1960, Americans had become fully aware of the new Africa, but they did not know what to make of it, because their preparation for Africa's explosion into the news headlines had been so much shorter and shallower than for the earlier emergence of the Far and Near East, or for the prominence of Latin America. The questions asked about the new African states were similar to those asked about other areas of topical interest:

Why do they vote against us in the United Nations?

Will communism take over in Africa?

Are these countries really prepared for independence and nation-hood?

Will they be so many more drains down which the United States will pour its economic and military aid, only to have them turn neutral-ist or communist in the end?

Do these new nations have the kind of history, social structure, and economic potential that Americans generally consider conditions for the growth of democratic government?

If these prerequisites are lacking, as they seem to be in most of the new states, what are the chances for the rise of totalitarian dictators, who will deal ruthlessly with their domestic opponents and naïvely with the forces of world communism?

In short, what are the prospects for Africa?

Approaches to the Study of Africa

Similar questions had been asked about the other areas, awareness of whose development had begun to dawn upon American opinion since the end of World War II and the start of the Cold War. But because of a longer and deeper preparation, a greater number of more experienced authorities could be turned to for answers to such ques-tions about Asia, the Near East, and Latin America. When they were asked about sub-Saharan Africa, these questions had to be answered either by journalists or by scholars. The journalists were concerned with the news of the day, which they usually reported to the best of their understanding. But their understanding was in terms of the categories and concepts forged by their non-African experience. When there was any violence between different factions in the Congo, they forecast the imminence of "civil war." Their American audience, about to celebrate the centenary of the great Civil War, projected memories of that epic struggle upon Congolese events, which were in fact of a quite different order. When the civil war did not take place, when other predictions based upon "news" failed to materialize, the interested American public became confused. Then scholars of African affairs—"Africanists"—were expected to clear up the confusion.

In the academic community, three professions especially were singled out to provide the answers: historians, anthropologists, and political scientists. Because of the uniqueness of the new Africa, the conventional approaches of these academic disciplines have unfortunately been mis-applied at times to the study of Africa.

History. Some diplomats and many historians of non-African backgrounds believe that a thorough study of their early history is necessary for gaining a proper understanding of the present and future of the new African states. These historical studies would have to be based at least in part on archaeology. According to this approach, for example, we would have to study the medieval Muslim kingdoms of West Africa to put current events in Ghana, Nigeria, and Mali into proper perspective. Some pronouncements of contemporary West African politicians seem to confirm this belief. Ghanaian, Nigerian, and Mali politicians do occasionally try to identify themselves with these kingdoms of a dimly recalled past—even though, in Ghana's case, the medieval kingdom of that name was nowhere near Nkrumah's Ghana, and was an Islamic state, unlike modern Ghana. Both before and after gaining independence, African independence movements have sponsored much history writing. These attempts to create a "national history" resemble efforts by some Americans in the last century to fabricate traditions, pedigrees, and ideologies sufficiently old and politically relevant to compete with their European models.

In Africa, the creation of history is even more artificial than it used to be in the United States, because *written* traditions, that is, true history, are of such recent vintage in most of Black Africa. Orally transmitted traditions are usually much older, but can never have the same impact as historical literature on the political movements and practices of modernizing communities. These communities are almost always led by their most literate, most educated members, who enjoy the highest prestige. Witness even the atavistic Mau Mau movement in Kenya. According to the British court which sentenced him, it was led by the most educated Kenyan of his generation, Jomo Kenyatta. When Africans try to exhume their "histories," they usually do so in defense against European critics of their independence drives. For example, "white settlers" tell them that they are unqualified to govern themselves because they lack the history which prepared the British or the Belgians for self-government. Or a colonial power tries to justify its rule by virtue of a "right of conquest," as in Southern Rhodesia, or pledges of allegiance to Queen Victoria made by tribal chiefs toward the end of the nineteenth century, as in Nyasaland and Uganda. In defense against such arguments, African politicians often search for, and by one method or another produce, purportedly historical counterclaims.

Otherwise, Africans in general are the most present-minded people on earth. African history, as studied by conventional historians, is of interest only as the history of European penetration and colonization of the continent. Their own pre-colonial history is of no interest to the Africans themselves. Without significant exceptions, all African leaders —from Dakar to Dar-es-Salaam, from the Cape to Kano—share the passionate desire to acquire all the good things which western civilization has produced in the two millenia of its history. They want especially to get the technological blessings of American civilization, and to do so as quickly as possible. The lack of historical consciousness of their peoples gives the African leaders a great advantage in moving rapidly toward this goal of modernization. They are not encumbered by written traditions, or by the visible and tangible physical presence of the ruins of their own "civilized" past—as most Asians have been. Therefore, they do not have to reconcile every innovation with the different practices of their past. The only past that they remember is the hated immediate colonial past. They want to move forward, away from it, as fast as they can. As outsiders who are trying to gauge the prospects for the new Africa, we can learn from its past in the main only in this negative sense. In other respects, paying too much attention to history would distort our perspective.

Anthropology. Before the eruption of modern politics, Africa was almost like a hunting ground monopolized by anthropologists among the social scientists. Some of them tended to view it as one vast reservation, on which *hos anthropos* was kept in his primeval state to enable anthropologists to study him—and then to tell the rest of us what our own primitive forefathers were like. The implication was, of course, that *we* had made tremendous strides. For their own purposes, many anthropologists did excellent jobs, but for our purposes today their approach to the study of Africans sometimes seems condescending and backward-looking.

Nevertheless, the anthropological approach still colors much contemporary western work on Africa. This is so because, until a short while ago, hardly anyone but anthropologists had been on the ground, or "in the bush." But how much will a good study of age groups among the Kikuyu tell us about the future of Kenya? It probably does not tell us enough even about the last five years in Kenya, where urbanization and other aspects of modernization have brought into being organizations like trade unions. These necessarily consist of members of different tribes, not Kikuyus only, and they could hardly operate on the basis of age groups, though echoes of these older forms of association may survive in the new ones.

Such echoes are important with regard to certain political procedures that the modernizing communities are developing. In this connection, a few anthropological studies, like Professor Max Gluckman's *The Judicial Process among the Barotse*, can be exceptionally helpful. Many

African societies have had highly sophisticated judicial systems that developed procedures of deliberation for the settlement of conflicts, which may be adaptable to the needs of modern polities. When we approach the study of the new Africa by way of older patterns such as tribal judicial processes, we must always bear in mind that these *are* being adapted and modified by the modernizing communities, where these are not trying to go completely western and get rid of everything traditional, in order to replace it with purely western forms. Except again for defensive reasons, no African will try to find the origins of democracy in the jungles of two thousand years ago—as German anthropological historians claimed to have found them in the Teutonic forests, or other western theorists in the Greek city-state, the Roman republic, Jerusalem, or elsewhere. Africans do not care where ideas or institutions come from. They do care where they, the Africans, are going and how best to get there.

Political Science. Some political scientists are deceived by this disregard for history and ancient customs into adopting another extreme approach to the study of contemporary Africa. They look at constitutions, legal documents, party systems, and election returns. They compare these data with what they are used to from the United States or Europe, judge what they find in terms of western standards, and then often find the newly self-governing African countries wanting in most respects. Where the anthropologist sometimes seems to have a professional vested interest in preservation of the *status quo,* perhaps even in its restoration, this type of political scientist (if the painter may draw a caricature of his former self) prefers to assume that there was nothing before the introduction of modern western political institutions: nothing except the "noble savages" of whom Jean-Jacques Rousseau wrote, endowed with the *tabula rasa,* the blank-slate mind, and roaming through the "empty places" made familiar by John Locke. These noble Africans are, of course, eagerly waiting for the political scientist to supply them with his own Utopia, which is the very model of the modern constitutional democracy.

In fact, the Africans usually turn out to be neither unusually savage nor unusually noble. Their minds are blanker than those of people in Europe or the Americas, with whom our political scientist is familiar, mainly in the sense that they are less resistant to innovation. The political scientist usually tells them to copy the wrong western institutions, for the wrong reasons, and by the wrong methods. His conclusions too easily "write off" to international communism a new state that does not have the tripartite separation of powers or a "two-party system." If we approach the new Africa in this way, any more or less stable pattern of politics that may be evolving eludes us, and we arrive at wholly misleading answers to the questions that Americans are asking about Africa. On the other hand, the writings of most European students of colonial administration and related matters cannot be of much help, because they worked more or less in the service of the colonial powers. As a result, they concentrated on the apparently static aspects of "native" society, which could be manipulated in the interest of the European administration. These shortcomings of conventional approaches have led a number of American scholars to try to develop new methods for the study of African affairs, which would at the same time facilitate understanding uniquely African features, and make possible comparisons with similar phenomena elsewhere. Those engaged in this effort seem to be in general agreement, regardless of their own particular academic discipline, that the first object of their study should be the *politics* of the new states, both before and after independence.

The Primacy of Politics

"Seek ye first the political kingdom, and all other things shall be added unto it." These words are inscribed on the pedestal of a statue of Kwame Nkrumah, "Founder of the Nation," that stands in front of Parliament House in Accra, the capital of Ghana. The statement, obviously an adaptation of the Biblical text about the kingdom of God, shows how African politicians frequently convert Biblical language to their own needs and thereby harness the prestige of Christianity and of education, brought by mission schools, to their drives for independence. But President Nkrumah's dictum does more than adapt a Biblical text to the needs of Africa, as he saw those needs. It also repeats, in more popular, more easily understandable language, an assertion made by the founders of the study of politics. Plato and Aristotle called politics the "master science," a statement which must have sounded like a truism to their Athenian contemporaries. The most important events in the lives of members of the *polis,* citizens of the city-state, were but consequences of events in the life of the *polis* itself. Those events, if they had not been caused by occurrences in nature—which in those days lay quite beyond human control or influence—were decided through politics. Hence politics was considered the queen of the sciences in ancient Athens. Today, when so much more in society, nature, and even the universe, can be subjected to deliberate human control or influence, politics is again becoming the most important human activity. This is especially true in Africa. In this sense, Dr. Nkrumah's commandment could well serve as the motto of any study of sub-Saharan Africa in the 1960's.

On the other hand, economics is often considered the most important matter in most African territories today. Their basic problems, as an "objective" outside observer would see them, are economic: poverty, hunger, disease, lack of transport, communications, and schools. However, this view repeats the mistake made sooner or later by every colonial power in Africa—made most dramatically so far by the Belgians in their Congo. The mistake consists of assuming that you can get people who are not governing themselves interested in improving their "general welfare," to use the phrase from the Preamble to the American Constitution, without *first* interesting them in politics. This cannot be done, and for a fairly simple reason. Economic problems that seem clearly most important to us, members of the "affluent society," may never occur to the ordinary African—who is referred to, not as the "man in the street," but the "man under the tree." A tribe living in dire subsubsistence poverty may not be aware of its misfortune, or of the possibility of what we call "economic development." Its members will recognize neither the problem of poverty, nor the goal of improvement, unless someone tells them about their misfortune, gets them to understand the nature of welfare, and explains to them means of approaching this goal. The explaining has to be done in a convincing manner, both popular and dramatic, that can be found only in politics.

In Africa, this process began in the latter years of World War II. At that time, almost all of the sub-Saharan territories were colonial dependencies of European states. It was therefore only natural for new African leaders to popularize the new goals through the issue of independence. They did this even where a paternalistic colonial administration began on its own initiative to solve the economic problems, as in the Belgian Congo. As soon as opportunities for economic advancement became available to some Congolese, their horizons expanded and they lifted their aspirations to higher levels, so that they, too, wanted to seek the political kingdom first. In other colonies, once the leaders (if not the followers) had become fully aware of this primacy of politics, no one would let himself be persuaded of the "objective" primacy of economic problems any longer; another inscription on the Nkrumah monument proclaims that it is far better to be poor but free than rich but unfree.

The Novelty of African Politics

To find answers to the urgent questions being asked about Africa today, we must, therefore, study primarily the pre-independence and post-independence politics of the new states, not their economics, history, or anthropology. Nor must we approach African politics as though it were European or American politics, if we want to avoid misleading answers. This is not meant to assert that there is something unique about the political *process* in the new African systems. But there is something very novel about the environment within which this process takes place, an environment very different from the sovereign nation-state, which has until recently been the principal focus of political science. Students of politics have been so preoccupied with this type of institutional structure, that most of them seem to take for granted, explicitly or implicitly, that politics can take place only within or among such states; in other words, politics must be either "national" or "international."

Until the rise of politics in Africa south of the Sahara, this had been a realistic assumption for the past century. Sovereign nation-states have been the main actors in politics. These states have typically been characterized by three main attributes: centralized force, territorial frontiers, and cultural homogeneity. The means of organized violence—army, police, judiciary, bureaucracy—have normally been controlled from one central point within the state. Some political institution had "the last word" and the means to implement this final decision: this is usually taken as the essence of sovereignty. The modern state has also normally consisted of geographically contiguous territory and been divided from its neighbor states by clearly defined geographical frontiers. Most modern wars, in the course of which each state brings to bear its monopoly of the means of force, have been fought over boundary issues. Finally, the population of the state has usually been made up of a "nation," whose members either shared a common culture and historical consciousness at the time of the founding of the nation state, or were subjected to deliberate internal cultural integration, and equally deliberate cultural differentiation from their external neighbors, subsequent to this founding. Students of politics therefore generally concentrate upon aspects of the "power struggle" within or between states. They gauge power in terms of military strength and its economic basis, as deployed within or across geographically defined areas, and as supported by the commitment of a nationally—or nationalistically—conscious population.

Under international law, all sovereign states are formally viewed as each others' equals. The existence of the international system of equal sovereign nation-states naturally shaped the goals and aspirations of independence movements in Africa. Ghana in 1957 became a sovereign state, with all the formal attributes of sovereignty that France has had for centuries. This is true of more than a score of former colonial territories south of the Sahara. However, these formal facts have not given Ghanaians or Nigerians, whose very names are usually of very recent coinage, either consciousness of a common past or cultural homogeneity.

The populations of these new countries have no memories of the military exploits of nation-building, which the peoples of almost all the older nation-states do have. Ghana formed a "union" with Guinea, although the two countries are separated for hundreds of miles by the Ivory Coast, and Sierra Leone and Liberia also lie between them, and although Ghana's official language is English and Guinea's French. The Republic of Mali was added as a third member of this union, and its territory again is nowhere contiguous with that of Ghana. The population of none of the new African states is culturally homogeneous. Many tribes are scattered all over the map, throughout several of the past or present territories of European powers that erected these "artificial cages" of colonialism on the model of the sovereign states whose dependencies they were.

These are some of the reasons why completely novel types of political association may be coming to life in Africa. These are not likely to resemble either states, or nations, or even federations, in the conventional meaning of these words. But if we were to look at the new African polities as though they were mere copies of sovereign nation states, then we would misunderstand these developments. Not only would we misunderstand them, but foreign policies toward Africa based on such distortions would probably contribute to thwarting this growth of something new, by treating the new systems as diseased aberrations only because they do not fit into any of our already archaic constitutional categories. To prevent this tragedy should be one of the principal purposes of the student of African politics today. Not only Africa but the whole of mankind urgently needs new constitutional forms to replace the obsolescent sovereign nation-state which leads us, among other things, still to worry about the integrity of territorial boundaries on the threshold of the age of seeing-eye satellites.

To the constitutional history of mankind, Europe contributed the sovereign nation-state. America contributed an absorptive, stretchable, flexible federal constitutionalism. Asia contributed nothing new. We may hope that Africa may contribute new forms of political association, which may yet help all mankind to avert the extinction with which the obsolescence of our political institutions is threatening us in our time. Whether Africa will make this great contribution, and whether those of us who live outside Africa will recognize and avail ourselves of it, if and when it is made—all this and much more will be decided by politics. In this sense, President Nkrumah's dictum has validity far beyond the continent to which he addressed it.

Chapter II

The United Nations and Africa

*We are at a turn of the road where our attitude will be of
decisive significance, I believe, not only for the future of this
organization but also for the future of Africa. And Africa may
well in present circumstances mean the world.*

—Dag Hammarskjöld

African "Nationalism"

The impact of international politics upon Africa, and Africa's explosion into international politics, both illustrate differences between
the new African political systems and the national states with which we
are familiar. Use of the term *international* incidentally shows how our
thoughts and judgments, and even our descriptions of events, are shaped
by the words we are in the habit of using. "International politics" today
is not conducted between or among nations, nor in its most important
phases even between states. Yet we suggest that this is in fact the case,
every time we use these words. The resulting distortions are even greater
when we speak of international politics in Africa, or of "African
nationalism."

When Frenchmen, Italians, Germans, or Czechs were building their
nations in Europe, they knew fairly well whom they wanted to include
in, and whom they wanted to exclude from, the figurative magic circle
that was to be drawn by their national (as distinguished from dynastic)
boundaries. Italians did not, at the same time that they were fighting
for independence from Austria, France, or Spain, attend Pan-European
Congresses together with Frenchmen, Germans, Spaniards, Czechs, and
other "nationals." Their representatives did not "lobby" delegates to

the Congress of Vienna or of any permanent European international organizations. The African independence movements, by contrast, have followed the reverse methods. African independence movements have not known exactly whom to include in the boundaries of their territories, unless it be simply those people who happen to be living there at the time of independence. But since boundaries were in the past regarded as meaningless barriers set up by Europeans to hinder the freer movement to which the Africans had been used before the coming of colonialism, or as obstacles designed to separate tribal relatives from each other, newly self-governing Africans are likely to consider boundaries less important than Europeans do. African independence leaders have been attending Pan-African Conferences both before and after achieving independence within their several artificial colonial cages. Their representatives have also been lobbying in the United Nations, and after independent African states themselves constituted a sizeable "voting bloc" in the General Assembly, they used this position to apply pressure to the remnants of colonialism in Africa.

African independence movements have, therefore, not been "nationalist" in the sense that European national movements have been or still are today. (Leaders of a Macedonian national movement periodically write letters to the *New York Times*.) The contrary is not proved by use of the word *national* in the titles of African political organizations, e.g., the various African National Congresses, *Mouvements Nationaux Congolaise*, the United National Independence Party of Northern Rhodesia, or the National Democratic Party of Southern Rhodesia. These titles only show that the Africans want to be modern—and to be modern means to become something called a nation, to be democratic, and eventually to establish a republic. Use of the label "national" also suggests that these Africans have been so much preoccupied with gaining their own independence or, after its achievement, with the independence of the rest of Africa, that they have not yet had the time to think ahead to the problem of the most suitable forms of political organization for their growing communities, at least not in theoretical or conceptual terms. This failure to theorize about their own future institutions, however, does not mean that the leaders of independence drives want only to create nations on the conventional pattern, or to transfer mechanically to their countries the political institutions of Europe or America.

The Impact of the United Nations on Africa

Mechanical constitutional copying of this kind occurred only in American-sponsored Liberia, which could at no time be described as a

successful constitutional democracy. But Liberia was the only independent
state that existed in Black Africa immediately before World War II.
Ethiopia had just been conquered by Italy on the second attempt.
Italy's first effort to acquire this colony had resulted in the most disastrous military defeat suffered by any European state at the hands of
Africans, in 1896. However, when the Negus, or Emperor of Ethiopia,
as a member of the League of Nations, asked that organization for protection against Italian aggression, the League proved completely impotent.

By the end of 1960, the following twenty states from Black Africa
were members of the United Nations: Cameroon, Central African Republic, Chad, Congo Republic (Brazzaville), Congo Republic (Leopoldville),
Dahomey, Ethiopia, Gabon, Ghana, Guinea, Ivory Coast, Liberia, Mali,
Niger, Nigeria, Senegal, Somalia, Sudan, Togo, Upper Volta. The very
fact that we "count" independent countries in terms of United Nations
membership is significant in itself. It shows how the organization of
world politics has shaped the demands and programs of African independence movements, as well as the structure and conduct of the
new political systems. In this process, the United Nations has played
a triple role. First, through its Charter and operations, the United
Nations simultaneously discredited practices of racial discrimination and
placed the seal of international respectability upon self-government as
the legitimate goal of dependent peoples. Second, it provided a central
meeting place and world forum for independence movements and their
leaders from all the colonial areas, including Africa. And third, the
United Nations assumed much more responsibility than its predecessor,
the League of Nations, for bringing independence to its own Trusteeship
Territories.

Non-Discrimination and Self-Government. The United Nations was
founded to celebrate the Allied victory over the Axis Powers. One of
these particularly, Nazi Germany, engaged in the most drastic racial
discrimination known to man—though most anthropologists disagreed
with the National Socialist concept of "race." Throughout World War
II, the Allies denounced these practices and made the abolition of racial
discrimination one of their main postwar goals. In one sense, this was a
bit paradoxical. After all, the two great English-speaking Allies had
always maintained color bar on a massive scale, the United States at
home, and the British in their Asian, Australasian, American, and
African colonies. And Hitler had taken at least some of his racial theories
from an Englishman, Houston S. Chamberlain. Perhaps the Allied
leaders denounced racial discrimination as strongly as they did partly
because Hitler had demonstrated the horrible extremes to which one
could carry the theory among white people, even though English-
speaking discriminators has usually thought of color as the essence of

race. Partly they were also appealing for the military support of colored peoples everywhere. In Asia this was expedient, because the Japanese were themselves colored. In Africa, both British and French colonial administrations recruited non-white troops for use in North African and South East Asian campaigns against the Axis.

Whatever their leaders' motives, the Allied populations became convinced, rightly of course, by the war-time anti-discrimination propaganda of their governments. As a result, they enshrined the condemnation of discrimination in the very Preamble to the Charter of the United Nations:

> WE, THE PEOPLES OF THE UNITED NATIONS, DETERMINED to save succeeding generations from the scourge of war, which twice in our lifetime has brought untold sorrow to mankind, and to reaffirm faith in *fundamental human rights,* in the dignity and worth of *the human person,* in *equal rights* of men and women and *of nations large and small,* and to establish conditions under which justice and respect for the obligations arising from treaties and other sources of international law can be maintained, and to promote *social progress* and better standards of life *in larger freedom,*
>
> AND FOR THESE ENDS to *practice tolerance* and live together in peace with one another as good neighbours, and to unite our strength to maintain international peace and security, and to ensure, by the acceptance of principles and the institution of methods, that armed force shall not be used, save in the common interest, and to employ international machinery for the promotion of the economic and *social advancement of all peoples,* HAVE RESOLVED TO COMBINE OUR EFFORTS TO ACCOMPLISH THESE AIMS.[1]

Racial discrimination was singled out for special condemnation elsewhere in the Charter. According to its Article 1, it is one of the "Purposes of the United Nations"

> To achieve international co-operation in solving international problems of an economic, social, cultural, or humanitarian character, and in promoting and encouraging respect for human rights and for fundamental freedoms for all *without distinction as to race,* sex, language, or religion.[2]

The same phrase, "without distinction as to race," is repeated in Article 55 of Chapter IX of the Charter, which deals with International Economic and Social Co-Operation, and in Article 76 of Chapter XII, which concerns the more directly relevant International Trusteeship System.

Since the United Nations came into operation, no international politicians—with the notable exception of diplomats and government

[1] Italics supplied.
[2] Italics supplied.

leaders of the Union of South Africa—have publicly advocated racial discrimination or the color bar. This constitutes a radical change from prewar practices. This change was naturally noticed by African politicians and made a tremendous impact upon them. This was particularly true of Africans who received some of their education in the United States or Great Britain, especially during the years of the war, when this international turning away from discrimination was rehearsed in the internal politics of these countries. The French had always had a better record in this respect, partly for what we might call psychological reasons (their lack of a "Puritan" tradition), partly because of their professed goal of total cultural assimilation of their dependent peoples. The French had demonstrated their good intentions by appointing a Negro from French Guayana, Felix Eboué, as governor in French Equatorial Africa at the beginning of the war. At the end of the war, in their usual centralist way, they legislated for at least apparent equality through direct representation of their African colonies in the national Parliament at Paris.

The French, as the British and other metropolitan powers with smaller holdings in Africa, also had to face up to the logical corollary of the Charter's anti-discrimination plank, namely the legitimacy of the goal of self-government. The Charter itself detailed this aim in its Chapters XI and XII, dealing, respectively, with a Declaration Regarding Non-Self-Governing Territories and the International Trusteeship System. According to Article 73,

> Members of the United Nations which have or assume responsibilities for the administration of territories whose peoples have *not yet* attained a full measure of self-government recognize the principle that the interests of the inhabitants of these territories are paramount, and accept as a sacred trust the obligation to promote to the utmost . . . the well-being of the inhabitants of these territories, and, to this end—
>
> (a) to ensure, with due respect for the culture of the peoples concerned, their *political,* economic, social, and educational advancement, their just treatment, and their protection against abuses;
>
> (b) *to develop self-government, to take due account of the political aspi-rations of the peoples, and to assist them in the progressive development of their free political institutions,* according to the particular circumstances of each territory and its peoples and their varying stages of advancement.[3]

Article 76 lays down the "basic objectives of the trusteeship system":

> (a) to further international peace and security;
> (b) to promote the political, economic, social and educational advance-

---

[3] Italics supplied.

ment of the inhabitants of the trust territories, and their *progressive development towards self-government or independence* as may be appropriate to the particular circumstances of each territory and its peoples and the *freely expressed wishes of the peoples concerned* and as may be provided by the terms of each trusteeship agreement;

(c) to encourage respect for human rights and for fundamental freedoms for all without distinction as to race, sex, language or religion, and to encourage recognition of the interdependence of the peoples of the world; and

(d) to ensure equal treatment in social, economic and commercial matters for all Members of the United Nations and their nationals, and also equal treatment for the latter in the administration of justice, without prejudice to the attainment of the foregoing objectives. . . .[4]

Not only these substantive provisions of the Charter of the United Nations, concerning the goal of self-government, but the whole tone of the document differs markedly from the parallel provisions of its predecessor, the Covenant of the League of Nations. The Covenant had nothing to say on the subject of racial discrimination. It confined itself to urging Members of the League, in its Article 23, to "undertake to secure just treatment of the native inhabitants of territories under their control." The term *native,* had, of course, become anathema to those described by it, by 1945, and even more so by 1960. The provisions of the Covenant dealing with League of Nations Mandates are even more revealing of the condescending and paternalistic attitude toward colonial peoples that prevailed in the Europe of 1919.

Article 22

1. To those colonies and territories which as a consequence of the late war have ceased to be under the sovereignty of the States which formerly governed them and which are inhabited by peoples not yet able to stand by themselves under the strenuous conditions of the modern world, there should be applied the principle that the well-being and development of such peoples form a sacred trust of civilization and that securities for the performance of this trust should be embodied in this Covenant.

2. The best method of giving practical effect to this principle is that the *tutelage* of such peoples should be entrusted to advanced nations who by reason of their resources, their experience or their geographical position can best undertake this responsibility, and who are willing to accept it, and that this tutelage should be exercised by them as Mandates on behalf of the League.

.   .   .

5. Other peoples, especially those of Central Africa, are at such a stage that the Mandatory must be responsible for the administration of the terri-

[4] Italics supplied.

tory under conditions which will guarantee *freedom of conscience and religion,* subject only to the maintenance of public order and morals, the prohibition of abuses such as the slave trade, the arms traffic and the liquor traffic, and the prevention of the establishment of fortifications or military and naval bases and of military training of the *natives* for other than police purposes and the defence of territory, and will also secure equal opportunities for the trade and commerce of other Members of the League.[5]

Apart from the mention of freedom of conscience and religion, there was no mention of anything approaching equal rights for members of all races or its corollary, advancement toward eventual self-government, independence from the Mandatory Powers, and full membership in the League of Nations. We can see how far publicly expressed attitudes on these matters had moved between 1919 and 1945. We should also remember that the United States, though President Woodrow Wilson had been one of the architects of the League of Nations, had not joined that organization. But it did become a charter member of the United Nations, which was founded in San Francisco, and whose headquarters became permanently located in New York City.

The Government of the United States, too, had to face the independence corollary of its declared commitment against discrimination. The experience of a Foreign Service Officer, Mr. Joseph Palmer, who later became the first American Ambassador to the Federation of Nigeria, illustrates changes in official United States attitudes on the question of self-government for the African colonies of our European allies. In 1947, the Department of State delegated this diplomat to represent it at the annual conference on colonial affairs held at an English university under auspices of the British Colonial Office. He had prepared a speech for delivery at the conference, in which he prodded the British Government to work faster on preparing their African territories for the eventual attainment of self-government. His speech had been approved all the way down from the Secretary of State himself. But just before he was scheduled to give it, the British chose this conference to announce a "crash program" designed to prepare the Gold Coast for responsible government within the Commonwealth over a period of twenty-five years. The American kept his prepared speech in his briefcase and instead praised the British Government for its realistic speed. Only ten years later, the same diplomat accompanied the Vice President of the United States as a member of President Eisenhower's special delegation to help celebrate the independence of Ghana. And three years after that, in 1960 —with another twelve years of the crash program still to run—he became the Ambassador to Nigeria, the most populous of Britain's African colonies.

[5] Italics supplied.

By 1947, the United Nations had not only been instrumental in making racial discrimination illegitimate and the goal of self-government legitimate for colored peoples; it had also declared illegitimate the use of armed force by sovereign states, internationally and, at least by implication, internally for purposes of repressing unenfranchised groups of the population. The speedy achievement of independence by the new African states is a remarkable fact, to which the United Nations contributed more than it is usually given credit for. Even more remarkable, however, is the very low incidence of organized violence in the course of the march toward independence. The colonial administration in every case enjoyed a monopoly of the means of organized force and, by using this monopoly, could have repressed the independence movement violently, had it wanted to do so. We will want to ask why the metropolitan powers "scuttled the ship of colonialism"—to use the disapproving phrase of Sir Roy Welensky—with relatively so little armed resistance. One answer suggests itself at this point: the ideology of non-discrimination and self-government. This doctrine had taken such a strong hold on the British Labour Party, that it set the whole process in motion by beginning the liquidation of the British Empire in India.

Meeting Place and World Forum. When delegates from India and Pakistan, other Asian, and, later, Near Eastern ex-colonies appeared at the widely publicized meetings of the United Nations, that organization began to provide a central meeting place and world forum for African independence movements, most of which had not yet been founded. An early instance of the United Nations' role as a world forum was India's attempt to apply pressure to the government of the Union of South Africa to desist from increasing and strenghtening discriminatory legislation against South Africa's Indian population. This attempt, which was repeated annually during sessions of the General Assembly, failed. So have efforts to get the Union to recognize the United Nations as successor to the League of Nations as grantor of the Union's mandate over South West Africa, which had been a German colony until World War I. However, such efforts at the United Nations are the only levers short of economic boycotts and armed force that outsiders have for publicizing their sympathy with the disenfranchised peoples of the Union and South West Africa, and, in later years, of the Portuguese colony of Angola.

Through mechanisms of this kind, the United Nations also affords the best forum for popularizing both the goals and the leaders of independence movements and newly independent states, especially in the United States, where UN headquarters is located, and whose people started off with the handicap of being less well informed about Africa than most European nations. The leading personalities from the various African countries naturally also get to know one another through attend-

ancc at meetings of the UN and its numerous subagencies, like the
United Nations Economic and Social Council and the World Health
Organization. These meetings in turn encourage the holding of other
conferences outside the United Nations itself. Such outside meetings are
often organized specifically in order to secure participation of groups that
do not qualify for UN membership, because they are not—or not yet—
sovereign states under international law. The Bandung Conference of
non-white peoples, held in 1955, is one example, attended by African
representatives from only Liberia and the Gold Coast. African examples
are several Pan-African Peoples Conferences that have met in Accra,
Tunis, and Cairo; Conferences of Independent African States, held
in Addis Ababa and Monrovia; and also the various independence celebrations, as well as ceremonies like Republic Day in Ghana. This function
of the United Nations has the one important result of giving changes in
one part of Africa a kind of chain reaction or wildfire effect all over the
continent. Because of their wide UN-sparked acquaintanceship, the
leaders are in constant touch with one another and even work out plans
of continental scope for their independence activities.

   Trusteeship Territories. Until July 1960, when it began to mount its
massive Congo operation, the United Nations had been most directly
involved in Africa through the Trusteeship Territories. Except for the
former Italian colony of Somalia which became a UN Trust after World
War II, the other trusteeship territories in Africa had been League of
Nations mandates that ceased to be German colonies in World War I.
The United Nations requires annual reports from the European states
that administer these territories. These reports are made to the United
Nations Trusteeship Council, on which newly independent ex-colonies
have had a voice from the beginning. The United Nations has prodded
the administering states to divest themselves of their responsibilities as
soon as possible. For example, when in 1954 the Council, on recom-
mendation of a visiting Mission to Tanganyika, recommended a twenty-
year target for independence, the British Government, among others,
condemned this proposal out of hand. Nevertheless, it proceeded to advance Tanganyika to full self-government and membership in the
United Nations by 1961! Of the sub-Saharan members of the United
Nations, Cameroon, Togo, Somalia, and Tanganyika are former United
Nations Trusts. They will soon be joined by Belgian administered
Ruanda-Urundi, and may eventually welcome South West Africa to
their midst as well. This territory was just mentioned as one of the two
main avenues of attack upon the policies of the Union of South Africa.
The South African Government has refused to admit Visiting Missions
of the Trusteeship Council to South West Africa, just as it has consistently denied the UN's competence over its treatment of Indians—or,

as for that matter, its shooting of Africans in the Sharpeville riots of March 1960. But Committees of the UN have made and published reports based on less direct information. The other trusteeship territories have regularly been visited by United Nations missions. As a result, more diplomats from outside Africa obtained more information about Africa in general than would otherwise have been the case. And African politics received a great deal of "free" worldwide publicity.

African Internationalism

What difference has the United Nations' triple role made for the domestic and foreign policies of the new African states? Most important, it has given these alleged "nationalists" a very internationalist orientation, an outlook that is directed particularly toward the United Nations. Together with other factors, the high regard in which African independence leaders hold the United Nations has also made them unexpectedly willing to forgo some of the conventional paraphernalia of state power and to reject, temporarily at least, the desirability of territorial aggrandizement and irredentism, as long as they can get the status required for United Nations membership. Since they invariably promise themselves a great deal from such membership—perhaps more than is realistic—they are in a great hurry to obtain membership for their countries. By the same token, after becoming members, they are reluctant to establish *formal* federations—on the model of, say, the American federal system—so that the representation of three or four member states of the new federation will not be reduced to UN representation for the one federation as a single whole. This attitude was a factor in preventing establishment of a federal Union of Central African Republics between the Congo (Brazzaville), Central African Republic, and Chad; and in breaking up the Mali Federation between Senegal and Mali (formerly Soudan).

To illustrate the high expectations of the United Nations that independence leaders generally hold, we can use their rejection of one of the major arguments employed to persuade Africans in Southern and Northern Rhodesia and Nyasaland to support the Federation of these three Territories. According to the pro-Federation argument, African Governments in Nyasaland and Northern Rhodesia would be able to help Africans in European-dominated Southern Rhodesia more effectively inside a continuing Federation, than if Nyasaland and Northern Rhodesia were to become separate independent self-governing states. In addition, supporters of Federation also argue that African politicians would have much more prestige as officers of the Federation than of the smaller states which now make it up. African politicians have rejected these arguments mainly because they believe that, if Nyasaland or Northern Rhodesia were to get independence tomorrow, its ambassador at the United Nations would be able to obtain independence for Southern Rhodesia the day after tomorrow.

Some western observers expected this commitment—indeed, this over-commitment—to the United Nations to be reversed as soon as the Africans' excessive expectations had been disappointed, as they were bound to be sooner or later. At certain points in the course of the Congo crisis, most Africans did seem to be disillusioned about the United Nations; e.g., over its failures to move against secessionist Katanga and to prevent the murder of Patrice Lumumba. But none of the African leaders ever gave up his basic support for the UN. Even Lumumba himself, as President Kasavubu after him, damned the United Nations one day, only to praise it the next and to cooperate with its representatives. And while President Nkrumah of Ghana condemned the Congo operation as a failure, Ghanaian troops continued to serve under UN command in the Congo, and a Ghanaian diplomat continued to carry on negotiations for the United Nations with Congolese leaders. When a large number of heads of independent African states held a conference in Monrovia, Liberia, in May 1961, their clearest, firmest resolutions urged continued support of, and action through, the world organization.

The role of the United Nations has also helped to make the newly self-governing states much less violent and much more legalistic politically than countries that gained their independence in earlier decades. None of the new African states achieved its independence as a result of the use of organized force. All of them made some use of the arguments for independence with which the Charter of the United Nations, a legal document, provided them. All of them were therefore committed from the beginning to using the kind of procedures that the United Nations could formally approve of. But, paradoxically, these are precisely pro-cedures which the founding members of the Organization, though they proclaimed their adherence to them in the Charter, have repeatedly violated since the founding in 1945.

The United Nations was established by, in the main, typical sovereign nation-states at the conclusion of World War II. These states, driven by their abhorrence of war produced by the six years of that global conflict, bound themselves to observe certain principles of international conduct, which were designed to prevent recurrence of that kind of war. But World War II had been produced by sovereign states, possessed of the conventional attributes of sovereignty—especially centralized con-trol of large armed forces, preoccupation with territorial boundaries, and a national or nationlistic population—have found it nearly impossible to obey these principles of international conduct. Meanwhile, however, their proclamation and popularization, along with the operations of the United Nations, have helped to bring into being in Africa south of the Sahara more than twenty new political systems. Under formal international law, these new units have to be regarded as so many more sovereign states. But they lack the essential content of the traditional nation-state. Moreover, their leaders are actually committed to the United Nations, because they believe it to be partly responsible for their attainment of independence. If the new African states became true copies of western—or worse, eastern—models, whose self-abhorrence created these principles of international conduct, then the new polities in Africa would not be able to stick to their commitment. But they still lack the military, territorial, and cultural substance required for exact copies. Their hope, and ours, may therefore lie in the possibility that they will evolve their own constitutional forms before they acquire the wherewithal to transform them into artificial copies of the now useless models of the Old World.

When the American Founding Fathers set about the task of perfecting the constitution of their union, they turned to the theory and practice of the Old World for counsel and illustration. The Federalist Papers, for example, contain many references to Montesquieu and Hume, the British Constitution and ancient leagues. However, it was not copying from foreign examples that made an outstanding success of the Constitution of the United States. Rather it was the authors' imaginative creativity that gave to this oldest of the still operating written constitutions its unique combination of stability and flexibility, of acceptability and efficiency. The most successful parts of the Constitution—its federal aspects, the Supreme Court, the amending procedure, the presidency—were not copied from models in the Old World, but created by inventive genius that applied itself to solving the new problems of the New World.

The novelty of the institutions they devised exposed the American Founding Fathers to strong criticism from Europe, even from their warmest sympathizers there. Similarly, today, as the new African countries are experimenting with new constitutional forms, their harshest critics from the Old World (which by now includes the Americas) concentrate on deviations from conventional and cherished devices. As a result, they may be doing the Africans in particular and the cause of constitutionalism in general a great disservice. They may also be thwarting positive contributions that the new Africans could make in the future.

Chapter III

The United States and Africa

I have great admiration for America's material achievements and regard for the democratic principles for which she stands, but I find it difficult to appreciate the eagerness with which many Americans holding public office pursue policies which can only have the effect of creating a vacuum in this continent.

Their motives appear to be compounded of determination to out-bid Russia and a belief that in backing racialism they will earn the gratitude and friendship of the African extremists.

—Sir Roy Welensky

The Problem for America

Until about 1957, both government and people of the United States showed little interest in Africa and were poorly informed about it. By 1960, more than a dozen American universities were operating African studies centers; many large foundations were supporting massive African programs; a number of organizations concerned with African-American relations had been founded; and new books about Africa were coming out daily in the United States without satisfying the reading public's hunger for more knowledge about the Continent and its peoples. United States diplomatic posts in Africa had been more than doubled in number and the scope of their activities continued to be widened.

Sub-Saharan Africa had suddenly become a problem for United States foreign policy and for the American people. In this chapter, we shall look for answers to three related questions: Why did Africa become a problem for the Americans during this particular period? What did the United States do about the problem? And how did people in Africa react to these American policies?

24

The Fear of an African Power Vacuum

Ever since the end of World War II, worry about defense against the Soviet Communist threat has provided the focus for almost all American thinking about foreign policy. This focus has often been shifted from one geographical area to another far removed from the first. It moved to Africa in 1960, when such a large number of African colonies became independent. Their independence meant the more or less complete departure of European "forces of law and order" from these territories. The question of who or what would replace these forces lay behind much of the newly generated interest.

This question was asked, and answered, in terms of a conception of world politics—indeed, of all politics—which enjoyed considerable popularity in the United States as a result of disappointment from the excessive expectations of "peace" that had been generated during World War II. Adherents of this view look on international politics as a "power game." By power, they understand military force and the resources required for the development, production, and maintenance of military force, including propaganda capacity. Their notion of power and their "model" of international relations tends to be mechanical rather than organic. That is why they use phrases like "balance of power" and "power vacuum." Just as, in the mechanistic view, nature was said to "abhor a vacuum," so, according to this view, it is in the nature of international politics to abhor a power vacuum. On this model, they interpret happenings in Africa along the following (slightly simplified) lines.

The European colonial powers are leaving Africa—a fact which, incidentally, cannot be attributed to any relative loss on their part, or to any relative gain on the Africans', of power prior to their departure. As a result, one or more power vacuums have come into being. Each vacuum must be filled by either one or the other of the two great power blocs in the world because, according to this view, there are only two such blocs. If the United States does not move in where its allies of the North Atlantic Treaty Organization moved out, the Soviet Union inevitably will. "Moving in" or "taking over" is thought of in military, economic, and political-constitutional terms. In other words, the argument is, first, that we need to take over the military bases of the departing colonial power. The West needs these bases, and if the United States fails to replace France or Great Britain, the Soviet Union will do so instead. Second, the United States should protect whatever investments Americans already have in the ex-colonies and, beyond this, it needs

Africa's raw materials and markets. If we do not keep these countries within the over-all economy of the West, they will become economically dependent upon the Soviet bloc and turn to socialism as the pattern for their domestic economies. This kind of reasoning lies at the bottom of most advocacy of economic assistance to "underdeveloped" or "developing" countries. And third, we should urge the new states to adopt western constitutional and political arrangements, like the tripartite separation of powers and the two-party system. Failure to borrow such western institutions will probably lead to the establishment of a totalitarian dictatorship of the Soviet Russian or, worse, Red Chinese type.

Each of these three arguments is usually based upon some fairly recent experience of American foreign policy said to be analogous to the current African problem at issue. The military argument, for example, can be expounded by analogy to the loss of China to the Communists, as it frequently is by Foreign Service officers who are still smarting under criticism of the Department of State for its unsuccessful handling of the Chinese problem. This particular analogy may seem rather far-fetched: Mao's army had been in existence for decades; China and the Soviet Union are contiguous; and the United States had been pouring enormous quantities of military help into Chiang's China. The case of the former French colony of Guinea is also frequently used in support of the military argument. Guinea was the only French colony to vote against membership in the new French Community in the referendum organized by General DeGaulle in September 1958, after the founding of the Fifth Republic. The French consequently pulled out in what seemed like a fit of petulance. They are said to have "pulled out" not only themselves, but as much equipment as they could lay their hands on, including telegraph wires and perhaps even light bulbs. Guinea's President Sekou Touré turned to other western countries, including the United States, for help. When he received no response, he accepted quickly proffered aid of, among other things, weapons and military and police "advisers" from Communist countries.

This "realist" interpretation also takes into account that the United States will be handicapped from the beginning in its dealings with the newly self-governing African countries, because the departing colonial powers are also fellow members of NATO. The Africans are therefore likely to resent efforts to replace European with American power. Efforts by the Soviet Union, in the course of the United Nations debate on the Congo, to identify not only the United States, but also Canada, with Belgium (the NATO ally) illustrate this difficulty. However, so the military argument concludes, American national interest demands that we replace colonial power in Africa, just as it demanded that the United

States replace British power in Greece and Turkey under the Truman Doctrine of 1948.

African independence leaders themselves often seem to be lending substance to the economic argument. They do this whenever they play the international game of "blackmail" for economic assistance. They tell the United States, in effect: "If you don't give us so many millions of dollars, we will know where to turn." After they have established contact with the Soviets, the African leaders probably tell them more or less the same thing. Many examples from outside Black Africa including Egypt, suggest that it is possible to play both ends against the middle. Nor have the Communists so far taken over any country, non-contiguous with territory already held by them, as the result of their response to appeals for economic aid of this kind. Guinea can again be cited, since it provided the Soviet bloc with its first opportunity in sub-Saharan Africa to render massive economic and technical help while the West was at a largely self-imposed disadvantage. Its President, Sekou Touré, is an avowed Marxist, who made official visits to both the United States and China. Guinea has concluded technical assistance agreements with China, the Soviet Union, and other Communist countries, but also with the United States. Guinea's aluminum resources are being developed by a consortium of western companies, in which an American firm has the largest share. According to its officers, relations between this consortium and Sekou Touré's government have been excellent. In Ghana, which has entered into commercial relations with the Soviet bloc, western trade and aid continue to be welcomed, for example in connection with the Volta River Development Project. In 1961, the United States Government delayed a loan for this purpose, partly out of resentment over President Nkrumah's apparent friendliness for the Soviet Union. Still, Ghana accepted a large contingent of American school teachers under the auspices of the Peace Corps.

The constitutional-political argument is usually illustrated with cases taken from postwar experience in South East Asia. There, with the possible and perhaps only temporary exception of India, neither efforts to introduce western institutions, nor attempts to create new indigenous constitutional forms have been markedly successful. When President Sukarno of Indonesia, a leading neutralist and host to the Bandung Conference, began to experiment with his system of "guided democracy," Secretary of State Dulles condemned this as smacking of totalitarianism. Similar denunciations were later made by lesser American authorities of Ghana's republican constitution of 1960, and of Dr. Nkrumah's handling of his opposition both before and after its adoption.

These critical interpretations of developments in Africa south of the

Sahara are explicitly or implicitly based, as suggested above, upon a certain model of world politics and a certain concept of power. Both the model and the concept seem more static and more mechanical than the realities of contemporary politics demand. These realities include modern weapons systems and increasing popular opposition all over the earth to the use of armed force. Adherents of this view tend to look upon the world as divided into two opposing camps, precariously balanced in a "balance of power." The transfer of a little more population, territory, and resources from one side of the scales to the other is expected to determine defeat or victory.

Instead of thinking of world politics in such mechanical terms, we might think of it as a vast, complex, constantly expanding network of electronic communications. In this network, the United States and the Soviet Union send the heaviest volume of "messages." But these two "super-powers" are not the only broadcasting stations hooked up with the global network. If they were to overload the system, wires would burn up and some, if not all, receivers would explode. The point is that there are many other large and small stations in the grid, all of them are connected with the United Nations, which we might think of as a kind of central switchboard. The new African states are still relatively insignificant, when taken individually, in terms of their use of the network and the volume of messages that they can either send or receive. Their generators are new and need booster shots in order to turn over for the first time. They are new models, still being designed and redesigned by a method of trial and error for the new tasks that they will have to perform.

This electronic model of world politics also suggests that world politics today is not only a matter of applying power, i.e., force, at certain points in order to move the target of one's attention in the desired direction. It is also a matter of sending out signals on a wavelength on which the target can receive them, will understand these messages "loud and clear," and is likely to respond to them in the desired fashion. In other words, the United States and even the Soviet Union want not so much to force other countries to do their bidding, as to elicit their consent. With this notion of world politics in mind, we should now take another look at the three arguments over power politics in the new Africa.

The Military Problem. The military conception of Africa as a problem for the United States makes the least sense of the three. It is being advanced with decreasing conviction and frequency, because the United States can no longer be said to need even those bases of the Strategic Air Command which it had been operating in North Africa for a number of years. The fact that development of intercontinental ballistic missiles, of the Polaris that can be fired from submerged submarines, and of other weapons systems has made bases of this kind superfluous, takes the ground from under proposals to secure new military bases in the new states. We should welcome the waning of the military argument in view of the lack of military traditions in these new political systems, which has already been mentioned as a novel phenomenon in modern history. No independence movement in a still colonial territory hopes to achieve its independence by military means or through the use of other kinds of organized force (with the possible exception of the Portuguese colonies). None of the top leaders in sub-Saharan Africa rose to prominence by way of a military career, except in the Sudan, which is usually considered a part of the Middle East. The level of armed force in all of Black Africa—with the exception of Ethiopia, which is not a new state—is relatively very low. For example, in 1960, Ghana's expenditure for this purpose was less than two per cent of the gross national product. Even if this is doubled, as planned, the proportion spent for military ends would still be far lower than in most of the rest of the world, and especially in the countries that are members of the two great power blocs.

Some European colonialists reject this kind of reasoning. They assert that "the African" has respect only for strength and force: if the West does not show its power, the Communists will show theirs, and the African countries will join the other camp. However, all the recent experience of the colonial powers in Africa suggests that Africans generally do not respect power in this military and police sense. In every case, the colonial power had a total monopoly of the organized means of violence. The leaders of the independence movement had no power at their disposal at all. But these leaders personified and symbolized the consensus of their people in massive opposition to the colonial regime which had by then come to rest almost on force alone. In this situation, the metropolitan powers lost their nerve, the more so because of the postwar abhorrence of the use of force for political repression. The only colonial powers that did not give in to this kind of pressure from their powerless subjects in Africa were Portugal and Spain, whose home governments do not rest on consent.

The Economic Problem. Developments in the new Africa present problems of economic power for the United States, in four main respects: nationalization of American investments, withholding of strategic raw materials, economic assistance, and competition between capitalism and socialism. There has been relatively little American investment in Black Africa. American investment in heavy industry, especially mining, was concentrated in the Union of South Africa and on the Northern Rhodesian Copperbelt. During the war, the United States Government subsidized uranium mines in the Belgian Congo for use in the atom bomb. Fear of nationalization of private American investments is, again, often based upon analogies between contemporary Africa and other developing countries which reached "nationhood" and/or asserted their independence from foreign economic "imperialism" in earlier decades. Nationalization, according to this fear, will not only damage the investors (unless due compensation is paid in the exceptional case), but also lead to Marxist socialism, the inevitable forerunner of communism. This reasoning overlooks a number of cases in the recent historical record, in which neither of these consequences has followed so far; e.g., Mexico, Iran, or the United Arab Republic.

The fear of being cut off from vital raw materials makes better sense. In this connection memories of the European oil shortage which followed nationalization of the Suez Canal by President Nasser are more alive in Europe than in the United States. However, there are few such raw materials with which Africa supplies the United States, particularly since uranium has become "a drug on the market." Moreover, because the newly independent states are very intent upon developing their economies, they are usually eager for help in the exploitation of such scarce resources. They consider themselves at an advantage, if this help comes from parties to the Cold War, as already mentioned, and are therefore unlikely to deny the United States access to something which in effect constitutes one of the Africans' best bargaining points. The conventional economic power argument is most persuasive in situations where the United States refuses to give economic help on its own initiative, in response to fears of the kind under discussion. Then the African country concerned is driven into increasing dependence upon the Soviet Bloc, unless it is able to raise itself by its own economic bootstraps. Except in the temporary case of Guinea, however, the United States has never made such a denial of economic or technical assistance.

Nevertheless, some American opinion has been critical of economic aid to countries whose economies are moving toward, or are already under some form of, socialism. This view is related to the conviction that private free enterprise capitalism is an integral part of American democracy, a prerequisite for democratic government anywhere, and the most important difference between constitutional democracy and totalitarian dictatorship. That conviction, in turn, would make President Nkrumah's injunction read: "Seek ye first the economic kingdom, and all other things shall be added unto it."

This kind of reasoning seems unrealistic for two other reasons. First, it overlooks the more or less socialist constitutional democracies whom the United States numbers among its allies in Europe, like Denmark and Great Britain. Second and more important, it assumes that the

Africans themselves view the rest of the world as consisting of two irreconcilable power blocs, the Soviets and the West, between which they must choose in an absolute, definitive, "either/or" manner. In fact, neither the world outside Africa, nor Africa itself appears in this dichotomous form to most Africans. Since both Russians and Americans are white, have had no direct colonial involvement in their continent, and are living in modern industrialized economies, the Africans may perhaps be forgiven for failing on occasion to recognize differences between them as relevant to African purposes.

However, even if the differences between these two powers seemed greater, the Africans probably would still not consider them irreconcilable, as do most members of the two great camps. To Africans very few things appear as extremes which cannot ever be compromised. Matters which appear as opposite poles to westerners are more often seen by Africans as different shades that blend into one another along a continuous spectrum. This peculiarly African view of the world may be related to the fact that most Africans are not heirs to Greek dialectical logic, or to their natural environment, and to the judicial processes of some tribal societies. The in-again-out-again spectacle of Patrice Lumumba prior to his assassination, and the maneuverings among the other Congolese politicians following it, illustrates the prevalence of this attitude. Although the western press generally presented these proceedings as a farce, perhaps they could be understood in part as a manifestation of this outlook, involving an apparent inability to recognize the "oppositeness" of things, which comes so naturally to us. Lumumba, Kasavubu, Tshombe, Mobutu, Gizenga, Kalonji, Adoula, and the others could be more or less hostile and more or less friendly to one another, all at the same time; and they of course knew, or got to know, each other intimately.

We will return to this phenomenon later in this book, for example, when we discuss the failure of some former British colonies to adopt the British institution of the loyal parliamentary opposition. This refusal to recognize the—to us—apparent irreconcilability of East and West may also be connected with the relatively non-ideological, pragmatic way in which most of the self-governing Africans have been conducting their politics. Their pragmatic political style suggests, incidentally, a greater affinity between Africans and Americans, who usually pride themselves on their pragmatism, than between Africans and the ideological Communists.

The Constitutional Problem. Some journalists and scholars view the failure of new African states to adopt traditional western constitutional forms with the greatest alarm, because they expect it to upset the world balance of power in favor of the Communists. Such reasoning should be advanced with the greatest diffidence—though it often is in fact expounded with great self-confidence—by American political scientists, whose every effort in the past to transport specific American institutions, often inadequately understood by the transporters, to foreign soil has failed, and usually disastrously. However, even the British who, as we shall see, have been much more flexible in advising others about constitutional problems, have behaved in a similar manner. They have, it is true, not been as egocentric and ethnocentric as the French in urging the mechanical copying of their own institutions and procedures upon their former colonies. British-trained parliamentarians seem better prepared for the tasks of self-government than their French-trained counterparts, and this not only because the British usually started training earlier than the French. However, the British have often failed to realize that their former African colonies would, upon gaining their independence, have to deal with problems quite different from those, for the efficient solution of which parliamentary procedure at Westminster was designed or adapted.

At this point we need mention only one aspect of this typically British attitude: the parliamentary practice according to which every topic for debate has to be stated so that members of parliament are forced to vote either for or against it, and the related conduct of parliamentary politics as a battle between always and only *two* sides, the Government and the Opposition. This practice is of little use to a parliament most of whose members do not normally and habitually think in terms of mutually exclusive logical opposites; who represent a population the vast majority of whom are in favor of their Government's getting on with the one big job of modernization, under the leadership of the man who won the drive for independence.

The two-way oppositional pattern of politics can be positively harmful where it results in the exclusion from constructive political or administrative work of all supporters of the Opposition political party, when the whole country has only a handful of people with the education or experience required for this kind of work. Most Britons have been too shrewd politically to jump to the conclusion that any deviation from the Standing Orders of their House of Commons will lead the African deviationists to join the Warsaw Pact. But there have been some Americans who seemed to convey the impression, to Africans at least, that failure to adopt the American separation of powers would have even more dire consequences.

Nonetheless, the communist threat to the United States and its allies does exist even if it does not seem to loom as large in Africa as in other parts of the globe. But the nature of that threat is not primarily political in the constitutional sense just discussed, nor military, nor even economic. The United States is not likely to succeed in preventing communist expansion to Africa by power moves in any of these three directions. What is going on in sub-Saharan Africa, even in unsettled countries like the Congo, is less a struggle for power than it is a process of building consensus. From the point of view of the Soviets, their best bet would seem to lie in creating situations of more or less permanent instability in all areas. The United States would be playing into their hands by basing its African policy upon the mechanical power interpretation of events. For instance, establishment and support of a military dictatorship is bound to lead to alienation from the United States, once the dictatorship that rested on its support has been overthrown—as some have been overthrown among America's allies on other continents, where force is more respected than in Africa. Misunderstanding constitutional innovations will lead to the estrangement of their authors and the rest of the politically-conscious population of the country concerned, and thus to their readier acceptance of Soviet professions of sympathy. Finally, economic support, unless it is given very carefully and intelligently, can easily lead to very bad dislocations, such as in other developing countries have in the past often provided a wonderful climate for domestic communism to thrive in.

Parallels to the American Revolution?

Not fear alone, but also hope has stimulated American concern for the new Africa. Many Americans believe they can recognize a great deal of similarity between the American Revolution and the drama of independence struggles in Africa. This belief, for example, led citizens of Lexington, Massachusetts, to invite a score of diplomats from independent African states, along with the United States Assistant Secretary of State for African Affairs, to participate in Lexington's and Concord's annual celebration of Patriots Day, in 1961. Similar hopes had been entertained in the 1940's and 1950's about India and other Asian colonies when they achieved their independence. Americans saw the Indian struggle for independence from the British Empire as a repetition, or even a deliberate re-enactment, of a familiar American historical scene. When the political oratory or the constitution of a newly self-governing Asian country echoed a phrase from the Declaration of Independence or the Constitution of the United States (the former was, and is, used more often than the latter), Americans considered this a good omen. When subsequent conditions proved quite different from either the intentions or the results achieved by a Jefferson or Washington, many Americans were quite disappointed. Failure of the new states to follow through with a successful equivalent of the Constitutional Convention of 1788, the rise of dictators, the high incidence of civil disorder, especially in South East Asia, naturally served to reinforce American fears of the Soviet threat, should their initial optimism about apparent re-enactments of their own "movement for colonial freedom" be disappointed once more.

Disillusionment is likely to recur, if the parallels between the American Revolution and African independence drives are carried too far. There is little real resemblance between the goals, problems, and struggles of the thirteen colonies of Great Britain in the 1770's, and those of the assorted British, French, Belgian, Portuguese, Spanish, and Italian colonies in Africa in the 1950's and '60's. The Americans won their independence in a major war, in which troops on both sides fought under the leadership of experienced professional military officers. In the course of that war, deaths due to battlefield wounds on the American side alone amounted to 4,044, out of a total population of about 3,500,000, while the total casualties sustained by all involved were much higher. And there were no racial or cultural differences between Americans and British; and the racial and cultural differences between these "dependent peoples" and their colonizers are of course one of the main reasons for the desire for independence. The American colonists, it has been said, were fighting for *their* interpretation of the British Constitution, which they considered more valid than that placed upon it by the British Parliament. African independence leaders are relatively uninterested in the nature of their mother-countries' constitutions. The "constitution" which they cite to support their cause is the Charter of the United Nations. Most Africans are conscious of these differences. They usually do not turn to the United States when searching for independence struggles upon which to model their own, except perhaps when they are looking for some of the ideology of independence that has been elaborated in the United States in almost two centuries that have passed since the Declaration of Independence. For other purposes, India, Egypt, and after 1957, Ghana, appear to them much more suitable models, and quite logically so.

Leading American friends of the new Africa often seem quite unaware of this, as indicated by the Patriots Day invitation mentioned above. And while this kind of American hospitality is unlikely to do any harm, it suggests the feelings of ambivalence which complicate Afro-American relations on the side of the United States: its self-image of the revolutionary independence struggle leads many Americans to identify themselves with the presumed latter-day counterparts of Jefferson and Washington, the Adamses, and Paul Revere. But some of these same Americans are by now no more revolutionary than the Daughters of the American Revolution and aspire to be rather like upper-class Englishmen or their Continental European equivalents—who also happen to be the very colonial powers from whom the Africans have won or are about to win their independence. Moreover, these colonial powers are allies of the United States in NATO against the Soviet Bloc. Some are also allies in the South East Asia Treaty Organization, and because of the relative failure of experiments in self-government in that area, otherwise pro-African Americans fear similar failures in Africa, subsequent power vacuums, and the danger of Soviet acquisitions. Whether individual Americans are interested more out of sympathy for anti-colonialism or antipathy to communism, these two emotions have reinforced one another to attract a rather ambivalent attention to events in Africa.

American Negroes and Africa

The third reason for American interest, the American Negroes, makes for even more complex ambivalences. The first representative of the United Nations in the Congo was Dr. Ralph Bunche, its Assistant Secretary General and highest ranking official of United States citizenship. Dr. Bunche is also an American Negro, who a few years earlier had turned down President Truman's request that he become an Assistant Secretary of State, because he did not want his family to live in Washington, D.C., the nation's capital, where there is too much discrimination against Negroes. The existence of the American Negro community and of its slow triumph over vestiges of pre-Civil War days may well be the single most important reason for the current preoccupation with Africa. It is of course closely related to the other two reasons. Many white Americans have a guilt complex even now, many generations after 1776 or 1788, about the exclusion from freedom of slaves and their descendants, by the original States. At one point in the history of the United States, this feeling contributed to the founding of Liberia. At another more important point it contributed to the Civil War, in the course of which 365,000 died due to wounds in the Union Army alone—and it is significant that official military reference books still, a century later, do not give the statistics for the Army of the Confederacy. It took a vast number of casualties before it was established that a nation conceived in liberty and dedicated to the idea that all men are created equal could long survive.

A hundred years have passed since that war, but the descendants of the slaves liberated by it are still being discriminated against in many parts of the Union. The Communists, who profess to be the most thorough-going egalitarians of all—albeit nonbelievers in any "creation" of equal men—omit no opportunity to advertise remnants of discrimination against Negroes in the United States. The federal government's efforts to abolish discrimination have come about partly at least in response to this largely hypocritical communist challenge. It is conceivable that even the United States Supreme Court's decisions in the desegregation cases of 1954 might have been less clear, or not unanimous, had it not been for this atmosphere of the Cold War.

However, even before the Cold War and World War II, Negroes from both the United States and the Caribbean had been among the pioneers of what is now known as Pan-Africanism. To other American Negroes, the creation of independent states in Africa may seem as the culmination of the process of acquiring full respectability as an American minority group, like the independence of Eire for Irish-Americans and the founding of Israel for American Jews. Perhaps the Negroes had even more to gain than other minority groups because—unlike all others in the United States—they had had no "old country" with which to identify themselves. They had no Old World culture, or its specific religion, to transplant to the New World, to cherish, and to develop in its American setting. They had no language or literature through which to transmit old traditions to their children and children's children. In this sense, "American Negroes are the most American of all Americans," in Professor Clinton Rossiter's words. And when a Negro president, prime minister, or diplomat visits the United States, is received at the White House—perhaps having been refused service by a turnpike drive-in—interviewed on national television, or viewed at the United Nations, many American Negroes enjoy an unprecedented feeling of identification and pride. This recognition proves the falsity of what their detractors have been saying in order to maintain the barriers of discrimination. In its extreme form, this feeling led to an increase in the membership and public notoriety of Negro racist groups like the Black Muslims. Of course, African news can also have opposite effects on American Negroes, when it is full of reports of savage atavism, as in the case of Mau Mau, or of confusion and chaos, as from the Congo. Then some American Negroes react with shame or denials of any identity between themselves and their "cousins" across the sea.

In either situation, for all these reasons, the Negro community has also become a potential pressure group involved in the foreign policy process of the United States. In this respect, it may resemble some Irish groups that try to affect American policy toward Ireland and Great Britain, or some Jewish organizations that try to influence policy toward the Middle East and the State of Israel, and all the other hyphenated-American groups toward their respective countries of origin or of identification.

The American Response

If the Soviet threat, the self-image of anti-colonialism, and the existence of the Negro community are the main reasons for America's newfound interest in Africa, what has the United States been doing about it? What is its involvement south of the Sahara? This is hard to gauge, even where accurate figures are available. The answer depends upon the standard of comparison. Both government and private involvement was much heavier in 1961 than throughout the 1950's, and the rate of acceleration was constantly increasing. At the same time, there was much less involvement than in the other developing areas that had become trouble spots for the United States in previous decades. When compared with Soviet involvement, that of the United States, certainly if combined with that of the former colonial powers, was much greater. This was so not only because the colonial administrations had deliberately kept Russian representatives out of their territories, but also because the Soviets themselves realized the opportunities they might have in Africa even later than the United States started to think about the potential Soviet threat. For this Russian tardiness, there were both doctrinal and practical reasons, including Sino-Russian relations, too complex to be considered here. As of 1961, the combined communist diplomatic, economic, and cultural effort in sub-Saharan Africa was still considerably below its combined Western counterpart.

Until 1958, African affairs came under the Near Eastern desk in the Department of State. In that year, the post of Assistant Secretary of State for African Affairs was set up. At about the same time, the foundations were laid for a corps of African specialists in the Foreign Service. The number of United States posts in Africa has been increasing ever since, mainly in response to the "birth" of new states. The decision to establish a new diplomatic post was not always easy to make, as the case of Brazzaville, formerly the capital of French Equatorial Africa, shows. Until 1958, it was served by the American Consulate General in Leopoldville. After creation of the French Community, a consulate was set up to serve the four new member states of the Community that had come into being in French Equatorial Africa: Gabon, Congo, Central African Republic, Chad. The State Department was reluctant to convert the consulate into an embassy, for fear that this might give the Soviet Union and other communist states also a pretext for exchanging diplomatic representation. As it was, there were only four western consulates in Brazzaville. Nor did there seem to be any need for setting up separate consulates in each of the four states, especially since their leaders were negotiating to create the Union of Central African Republics. Even when Gabon dissociated itself from these efforts, this estimate was not changed. However, when all four became fully independent within the Community *and* were admitted to full membership in the United Nations, they expected to exchange ambassadors with the United States. In late 1960, the Consulate in Brazzaville was raised to Embassy status. Then Chargés d'Affaire were sent to the other three capitals, which received full-fledged American Ambassadors in 1961.

Until 1961, the United States Government provided relatively little direct economic and technical assistance to sub-Saharan countries. What little was given was sometimes very well applied: a forestry expert to one territory, an English-language teaching unit to another, and so forth. The World Bank, of which the United States is the most important backer, helped with long term investments, like its big loan to the Federation of Rhodesia and Nyasaland for the construction of Kariba Dam, the biggest on earth; or a much smaller loan to the Native Development Fund of Southern Rhodesia. Private American banks have been increasing their African commitments, as well as establishing branch offices. Other private American investments have also multiplied, as in the case of the aluminum and hydro-electric projects in Guinea and Ghana, or iron ore developments in Gabon.

At least as important as diplomatic and economic contacts has been American cultural liaison with Africa. African students began to attend American Negro colleges toward the end of the nineteenth century, and their number increased after World War I, especially in the 1930's. As a result, some of the most successful independence leaders, like Drs. Nkrumah, Azikiwe, and Banda, value American educational institutions more highly than do usually either the British themselves or their former charges. Starting in the mid-1950's, educational exchange was stepped up a great deal, on the initiative of both government and private foundations. As mentioned in the first chapter, American scholarships for students from Africa became an issue in the presidential campaign of 1960.

It was also during this campaign that plans for the Peace Corps were first popularized, usually in connection with Africa, since the American public happened to be more aware of African needs at that time than Asian or Latin American needs. Within half a year after the presidential election, the first Peace Corps contract had been concluded, with Tanganyika, for a road building team. One of President Kennedy's brothers had made a survey of African countries together with a Senate subcommittee. His brother-in-law, as head of the Peace Corps, also visited Africa. A Congressional subcommittee added a report on its trip to that of the Senate subcommittee just mentioned. The United States

Ambassador to the United Nations, Adlai Stevenson, asked the African states represented there to submit their specifications for the types of aid they required, only to be temporarily rebuffed by their spokesman, the Nigerian Ambassador.

The African Reaction

What has this American involvement gained us in exchange? This question has to be answered in two parts, one for Africans, the other for "Europeans," i.e., white residents of Africa, mainly in the Union and British Central and East Africa. The African reaction, to start with the vast majority, depends at bottom upon the level of education or, better, of plain information. Except in a few pockets of literacy, this level is generally so low that there is no reaction to America at all. People have not heard of it, or if they have, are incapable of distinguishing between one country of white English-speakers and another. Because of illiteracy, use of maps or globes for explaining the difference between the United Kingdom and the United States will not work. The employment of American Negroes to spread this basic public information would not help much in most situations, partly because many of them are relatively so light that Africans would consider them either whites or coloreds (of mixed blood); and partly because in countries still dominated by whites, life would be made very uncomfortable for them. Moreover, the use of Negroes for this purpose, or the mere mention of their existence and role in American society, often introduces a further element of possible misunderstanding. Since Africans naturally tend to project their local population proportions onto the United States, they find it hard to believe that American Negroes do make up only "One Tenth of the Nation" (the title of a book sometimes used by United States Information posts to illustrate this point abroad).

Better informed Africans, including some who have actually visited the United States, often have other misconceptions—or conceptions which are unfortunately accurate, but lead them to be less than friendly. One of the very few who had made a trip to New York at his own expense said of his experience:

> I flew to New York planning to travel all over your country. On the day of my arrival, a colored UN diplomat was "rolled" in Central Park. The next day, Negro children were mistreated in Little Rock, Arkansas. On the third day of my stay, my American hosts advised me against visiting Harlem in view of its high crime rate and the personal risk they and I would be taking. On the fourth day, I flew back to London. I hope I never have to go to your country again.

Little Rock and other resistance to desegregation naturally gives the
United States unfavorable publicity in Black Africa. So does discrimination against diplomats from the new African states, even if the President
of the United States subsequently makes a personal apology, as both
Presidents Eisenhower and Kennedy have had to do.

Occasionally, Africans condemn the United States for giving certain
types of financial assistance to countries not yet governed by Africans.
This happened in the cases of Kariba Dam and the Southern Rhodesian
Native Development Fund, mentioned above. Kariba was planned to
cement together two members of the Federation of Rhodesia and Nyasaland, Southern and Northern Rhodesia. Because of the Africans' massive
opposition to federation, many of their leaders resented American help
for this project. Some would, in any case, have preferred several smaller
hydroelectric projects, whose benefits would have been more widespread
in their opinion. Assistance to the Native Development Fund was interpreted by Africans to prop up the Land Apportionment Act. Under
this law, half the land of Southern Rhodesia was reserved for use by
Europeans, who made up one tenth of its population. Critics of the
American loan argued that by improving the poorer land reserved for
"natives," the United States would indirectly detract from the Africans'
claim to have the Land Apportionment Act repealed. Other Africans
have even swallowed Marxist arguments about United States imperialism; that is, they believe that the American government plans to make
the new African countries dependent upon the United States economically. Some of these misconceptions are due to the fact that few
Africans—and few Europeans, for that matter—understand the com-
paratively restricted role of the United States Government in the
United States, and the fact that private American individuals or organizations generally do many things entirely on their own initiative,
both at home and abroad.

The role of American diplomats is also misunderstood frequently
during the pre-independence period, when leaders of the anti-colonial
movements need help most urgently. American diplomats are of course
accredited to the very colonial government which the Africans are opposing. When African politicians come for direct help to them, they
have to be turned away, and this they sometimes resent. On the other
hand, Africans in Southern Africa appreciate the fact that American
libraries, operated by the United States Information Service, for many
years were the only nonsegregated public rooms within thousands of
miles. In the same vein, they resented repeated United States absten-
tions from votes to censure the Union of South Africa in the United
Nations, but were gratified by American votes against the Union, first
on the Sharpeville shooting in 1960, and against Portugal in 1961.

African politicians seem not to bear grudges for very long, a trait which may be related to their lack of a long historical consciousness. It means that the United States is in a position to overcome resentment of its spotty past record by treating representatives of the new states as equals, and by looking on their problems as truly theirs and not merely peripheral to American problems of the Cold War.

Although "Europeans" in Africa are normally better informed about the United States, their reactions to American policies are often much more simpleminded than those of the Africans. This, as we will see in the next four chapters, is largely due to the tremendous egocentrism of the white people remaining in the Union of South Africa, the Rhodesias, and Kenya. Those of them who are unwilling to make political concessions to African independence movements, even though they sense that their own days in Africa are numbered in direct proportion to such accommodation, tend to misinterpret all actions of others that come to their attention as directed against themselves. This almost paranoid outlook leads them, for example, to assert that the United States intervened against Great Britain in the Suez crisis only and deliberately in order to cause trouble for her remaining African territories. One Rhodesian politician even claimed that the Supreme Court of the United States rendered its decision against school segregation in 1954, only in order to make trouble for the whites of Southern Rhodesia! When a large group of elderly American tourists, traveling in a caravan of trucks and trailers, passed through Southern, Central, and East Africa, some white settlers dubbed them "Sudeten Americans," in an allusion to German "tourists" sent across the border into Czechoslovakia by the Nazis before their invasion of that country in 1938.

Among whites in Africa, the feeling is widespread that the United States is deliberately undermining the colonial powers with the intention of then moving into the power vacuum that will be left by their departure. Most of the colonial whites, and Afrikaners in the Union, are even more committed to the power interpretation of politics than is the school of political science criticized at the beginning of this chapter. To back such charges, they often point to Africans who have returned from trips to the United States on State Department sponsored "leader grants," or who have attended American universities, and who are said to be more "radical" than they were before this American exposure. They also resort to the economic side of the power argument, which is the white counterpart of black allegation of American imperialism. The United States, according to this reasoning, needs African markets, although consumer demand in Africa does not amount to much at present. As proof of this, the Europeans cite government-sponsored American trade missions that pay visits to these countries, mainly in order to help them develop their exports to the United States. The same charge is made when a mining company with heavy American investments pursues slightly more progressive policies toward its African employees than its competitor which enjoys no such backing. When the AFL-CIO helped to set up an African branch office of the International Congress of Free Trade Unions, under the leadership of Tom Mboya of Kenya, a white trade unionist accused George Meany, President of the AFL-CIO and one of America's staunchest and most outspoken anti-communists, of being a communist and of putting the United States Government up to inciting native labor against the white unions of Southern Africa. Yet this same move of the ICFTU was taken by African trade unions organized in West Africa under the leadership of Dr. Nkrumah as a blatantly imperialistic step of the capitalistic American labor leaders! It seems as though, in these periods of transition from colonialism to independence, Americans are damned if they do and damned if they don't.

In any case, the United States has to make decisions about its relations with the new Africa. Most resentment in Africa of specific American policies is based on inadequate or distorted information. Only a small part of this resentment is based on properly understood American policies. Most of these in turn are the result of American misunderstandings of this vast area and its peoples, in whom the American people became vitally interested only so recently and then very suddenly. To help Americans avoid such misunderstandings in the future is the main purpose of this book and especially of the following chapters, in which we shall be analyzing the politics of various regions and countries of sub-Saharan Africa.

Chapter IV

South Africa:
The Problem of Race

*As a basic principle of its attitude towards Natives and Coloureds
the Party recognizes that both are permanent parts of the country's
population, under the Christian trusteeship of the European races.*

—Program of the National Party

*The wind of change is blowing through this Continent. . . .
What we do today in West, Central and East Africa becomes known
to everyone in the Union whatever his language, colour or traditions.
. . . It has been our aim, in the countries for which we have
borne responsibility, not only to raise the material standards of life,
but to create a society which respects the rights of individuals—a
society in which men are given the opportunity to grow to their
full stature, and that must in our view include the opportunity of
an increasing share in political power and responsibility; a society
finally in which individual merit, and individual merit alone, is the
criterion for a man's advancement, whether political or economic.*[1]

—Prime Minister Harold Macmillan

The Politics of Petrified Memories

Black Africans in the new states show little attachment to the
few historical memories which they hold. Rather, they look to the
future. White Africans in the Republic of South Africa, descendants of

[1] From an Address to the Union Parliament, February 3, 1960.

43

the earliest permanent white settlers on the Continent, are fanatically committed to their many historical memories. They look to the past. The history of the Afrikaans-speaking white people of the Union is full of tragedy and bitterness that inhibits their realism about the present and leads them to move at the pace of classic tragedy toward their self-anticipated doom. This pace was set, in the early 1960's, by a slight majority of white voters, against not only the four-fifths of the Union's population who were nonwhite and therefore nonvoters, but also against world opinion, as expressed at the United Nations, where only diehard colonial states like Portugal refused to oppose South Africa's policies.

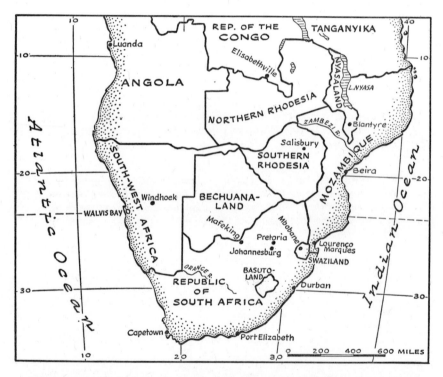

The Dutch East India Company established a station near the Cape of Good Hope in 1652. Because there were no Africans living on the Cape then, slaves were imported from other parts of Africa and from Southeast Asia. Today, descendants of the early Dutch settlers, and of Huguenots and Germans who joined them later, speak as their mother tongue a variation of Dutch called Afrikaans. They call themselves

Afrikaners, that is, Africans, and refuse to apply this term to Negroes, whom they refer to as Natives or Bantu (which means "people" in some Southern African languages, but is used as a racial category by the Afrikaners). All over the rest of Africa, individuals and parties are described as "nationalist" when they favor the independence of new states from European rule. In South Africa, members of the Afrikaner National Party, which came into office in 1948, call themselves "Nationalists," and are often referred to by their opposition as "Nats" for short. As a member of the Commonwealth, the Union gained full independence with adoption of the Statute of Westminster in 1931. The South African Nationalists wanted to refound a nation in which the Afrikaners would predominate over the English-speaking population, and to cut even symbolic ties with the United Kingdom and the British Crown by declaring the Union a Republic, as they did in 1961.

Most recent policy goals of the National Party are products of petrified memories of the Afrikaners' unhappy past. These memories have been interwoven with the Calvinism of their Dutch Reformed Churches into a comprehensive, consistent, and closed ideology that provides its adherents with answers to all questions and solutions to all problems, but which, if rigidly adhered to, leaves them little leeway for political maneuver. Among the most important memories are a relatively unpopulated land, in which organized African resistance was not encountered until about 1775, after which date it took a century of armed conflict in a frontier-like atmosphere before the Africans were confined to reserves; the British appropriation of the Cape at the end of the Napoleonic Wars, resulting in a series of "treks" into the interior by their forefathers to get away from British authority; the founding of Republics by these "Boer" forefathers in the Transvaal and Orange Free State; the Boer War of 1899-1902, in which they lost their independence and which brought British "concentration camps" among other hardships; the development of gold and diamond mining and, later, of a modern economy, controlled by British capital; the founding of the unitary, i.e., nonfederal, Union of South Africa in 1910, and its support of Great Britain in two World Wars, in which many Afrikaners sympathized with Germany; the crystallization of world opinion against racial discrimination after that War, especially in the United Nations, where South Africa found itself outvoted by increasing—and increasingly hostile—majorities on such issues as discrimination against Indians, administration of Southwest Africa, and the Sharpeville shootings of 1960.

Petrified memories of the earlier of this series of events became ingredients of the ideology of the Nationalist Party that came into office in 1948. South African racial and constitutional policy since that year can be understood best as a product of this Afrikaner ideology, whose sources therefore take on unusual importance. In Black Africa, the new politics has been pragmatic, not ideological. It has looked to the future, not the past. And it is experimenting with new constitutional forms, while South Africa is trying to revive old ones. These differences in orientation are as important as the related demographic fact of the presence of 3,000,000 whites in a total population of 15,000,000. This large white community, with its great internal cleavage between those who speak Afrikaans and those who speak English, has encouraged the study of South African politics with the methods usually applied to western political systems. Moreover, quite contrary to its Government's intentions, the Republic of South Africa provides a focus in opposition to which the independent black states to the north generate strong drives to form larger associations among themselves.

The Constitution and Afrikaner Ideology

When the Boers started their great treks away from the English on the Cape, they founded the republics of the Orange Free State and the Transvaal. These frontier communities were very democratic indeed; in some respects they resembled the Swiss *Landsgemeinde*. Their elected presidents, their laws, and their constitutions drew legitimacy from the *volkswil,* the people's will. This concept recalls Rousseau's general will, a resemblance not surprising in view of the orthodox Calvinism of the Boers and Rousseau's identification with his and John Calvin's hometown of Geneva. The concept, of continuing importance for Afrikaner ideology and Nationalist policy, contributed to misunderstandings between Afrikaners and Britons, to whose political theory and practice the notion of "will" as the source of law is quite foreign. The English-speaking peoples have generally assumed that law is not so much "made" or imposed by anyone's will, as it is "found" in custom and nature, and from time to time elaborated and brought up to date.

The Boer War was a clash of wills, in which Great Britain's prevailed because of her superior force. The British did not, however, force their Common Law upon the vanquished. Instead, the whole of South Africa (including Southern Rhodesia to this day) retained "Dutch Roman Law," which had been brought to the Cape by the Dutch colonizers long before the great codification of Continental Roman Law by Napoleon. As a result, judges have played as important a role in the development of the law in South Africa as in other English-speaking countries, and basic legal procedure continues to resemble that used in the United Kingdom and the United States. But the content and substance of the law has had wider scope, because its ultimate source was assumed to be the will of the "sovereign" people as successor to the imperial *potestas* of ancient Roman Law. This built-in contradiction between form and content, between procedure and substance of constitutional law erupted in the constitutional conflicts that preceded South Africa's reversion to republican government in 1961.

Seven years after the Boer War destroyed the Boer Republics, the South Africa Act of 1909 was hammered out between the enemies, on British initiative, but with participation by Boer leaders. The South Africa Act was passed by the British Parliament, like Canada's constitution, the British North America Act of 1867. Unlike Canada's, however, South Africa's constitution was not a federal one, instead combining the four provinces—Transvaal, Orange Free State, Natal, and Cape—in one union. The fact that the Union's Constitution was an Act of the British Parliament turned out to be important, because it meant that the courts could judge the constitutionality of bills passed by the South African Parliament in terms of a written document supported by the superior authority of an outside body, in contrast to the United Kingdom itself where, in the absence of a written constitution, Parliament itself is the highest authority and the last court of appeal.

Despite their participation in drafting the South Africa Act, despite the prominence of Afrikaners in the leadership of all major political parties in the Union since its founding, despite the international prestige—especially in both World Wars and at the founding of both the League and the United Nations—of their Afrikaner Prime Minister, Field Marshal Jan Smuts, many Afrikaners considered the Constitution of the Union and its link with the British Empire and Commonwealth an alien imposition. In this respect, they resembled the French Canadians of Quebec during the years before 1867, when the predominantly French-speaking and Roman Catholic population of Quebec and the predominantly English-speaking and Protestant population of Ontario were joined in a "forced marriage" under a unitary constitution. The British North America Act of 1867 substituted a federal system flexible enough to contain these cultural conflicts. Nevertheless, French Canadians' view of their country's participation in "Great Britain's imperial wars" has been almost as isolationist as the Afrikaners'—almost, but not quite, perhaps because the Roman Catholic ingredient of their nationalism maintains a link between French Canadians and the worldwide Roman Catholic Church, whereas the Afrikaners' Calvinism has been intensely egocentric ever since the Dutch Reformed Churches and their *predikants* (ministers) had been left to their own devices in the South African veld. In view of these parallels, some students have argued (with benefit of hindsight) that a federal instead of a unitary form of government might have provided the mechanism to resolve the

Afrikaner-English antagonisms. However, the argument overlooks South Africa's more serious cultural problem, the conflict between whites on the one hand, and the vast majority of Africans, Coloureds (people of mixed race), and Asians, on the other.

Boer and British attitudes toward nonwhite peoples differed from the very beginning, in part for religious reasons. The Dutch had introduced slavery to the Cape in 1717, where it continued as the basis of the economy until slavery was abolished throughout the British Empire in 1833. Under the influence of English missionaries, Coloureds in the Cape Colony were given the same legal status as Europeans in 1828. For the early Dutch settlers, according to Gwendolen M. Carter's excellent *The Politics of Inequality*, "The original distinction was between Christian and heathen. It was not long, however, before color became the index of status." [2] The Calvinist Boers drew heavily upon the Bible for justification of their racial policy, and their Afrikaner descendants today continue to do so. In this respect, they have sometimes seemed to display symptoms of the Lost-Tribe-of-Israel-complex, not unlike the Mormons'. The Bantu, according to some theologians of the Dutch Reformed Church, are divinely predestined to be and remain forever "hewers of wood and drawers of water" for the white elect.

Although the Dutch and their descendants always practiced some miscegenation—most frequently and most openly in the early days—the powerful religious leaders of their communities had to condemn this as contrary to God's Will. Indeed, from a theological point of view, they had to look upon the Coloureds as products of a particularly heinous variety of original sin. British extension of equal legal status and even the qualified franchise to the Coloureds of the Cape Colony therefore contributed to the decision of the Boers to trek into the interior. And as soon as Afrikaner Nationalists inspired by this ideology came into office as the Union's Government in 1948, they made removal of the Cape Coloureds from the electoral roll their first and most important goal.

From Union to Republic

Until they were able to address themselves to this problem, the Afrikaners proved very adept at working with British parliamentary procedures and the constitutional framework that the South Africa Act had provided. This framework was first used as the basis for local self-government by a partly non-British population when Canada was given "responsible government" after 1840. In the Union of South Africa, this

[2] Gwendolen M. Carter, *The Politics of Inequality: South Africa since 1948*, p. 18.

meant government by the King (or Queen) and the Union Parliament, consisting of the Senate and the House of Assembly. The British Monarch was represented by the Governor General who, until adoption of the Statute of Westminster in 1931, was appointed by the British Government. After 1931, the Governor General was appointed by the Monarch on nomination of the Union Government. Nationalist Governments nominated Afrikaner politicians to the position. Voters in the four provinces of the Union elected provincial assemblies that controlled certain local matters. But the provincial administrators—roughly equivalents of American state governors—were appointed by the Union Government.

The Union House of Assembly and Senate were elected, in the Orange Free State, Transvaal, and (with insignificant exceptions) Natal, by white men and, after 1930, white women. Before Union, the Cape Colony had had a "color-blind" franchise, partly reflecting the slogan of Cecil Rhodes, once its Prime Minister, of "equal rights for civilised men south of the Zambezi [the boundary between Southern and Northern Rhodesia]." Whites, Coloureds, and Africans had only to meet certain literacy and property qualifications in order to be registered as voters. To preserve this color-blind franchise, the South Africa Act provided, in one of its two "entrenched clauses," that no one should be disqualified in the Cape Province "by reason of his race and colour only," unless by a bill passed by a two-thirds majority of both Houses of the Union Parliament sitting together.[3] By such a majority, about 10,000 African voters were removed from the general voters' roll in 1936, and placed on a special Cape Native voters' roll, which elected three European members of the House of Assembly as Native representatives. In addition, Africans from all four Provinces elected indirectly, through a Natives' Representative Council, four European Senators. These changes were brought about while General James Barry Hertzog was Prime Minister in coalition with Field Marshal Smuts. Hertzog was leader of the National Party, Smuts of the South African Party which, upon outbreak of World War II, was renamed United Party, the label under which it became the Nationalists' official opposition after its defeat at the polls in 1948.

ᵽ All the most divisive issues of South African politics since the founding of the Union have been debated in terms of the cultural cleavage between Afrikaners and British. This has been true whether the issue was actually generated by this cultural conflict, or whether its real cause lay in economic or foreign relations problems. Memories of matters related to the Boer War aggravate ordinary economic issues, for example, because the major sources of income of the English- and

[3] *Ibid.*, p. 119.

Afrikaans-speaking populations differ, so that the dividing lines between economic strata usually overlapped with language and, therefore, with religious divisions. The same applies to issues arising out of the racial problems of South Africa, to the extent that more than one Afrikaner politician has said: "We have no Native problem—we only have the English problem." This is not meant to suggest that there was a great deal of difference, after 1948, between the racial policies of the Nationalists and the opposition United Party, which is supported by almost all the English-speaking voters and by only about 15 per cent of the Afrikaners. But the means by which each wanted to work toward solution of the Union's racial problems differed. This difference in methods seems more important than partial agreement on ultimate goals in this particular situation, the more so since neither party is likely ever to achieve the goals of its racial policy against the massive opposition of its own unenfranchised population and the outside world.

In South Africa, as in the United States though for somewhat different reasons, many questions of racial discrimination are ultimately converted into, and decided as, constitutional issues. In the years after 1948, the most lengthily and hotly debated constitutional issues have been concerned, in one way or another, with the franchise. This was true even of the referendum on the question of establishing a republic, held on October 5, 1960. In this referendum, Europeans in South-West Africa, technically not a part of the Union and claimed by the United Nations as a trusteeship territory, were allowed to vote, while Cape Coloureds were not. The very small Progressive Party, founded in 1960, used this discrimination for one of its major parliamentary attacks on the Nationalist Government's bill to hold the republic referendum. However, in this as in previous cases, disagreements on the franchise were only symptoms of much more basic disagreements about the very nature of the fundamental constitution of the country. These came out most clearly and most dramatically in the course of the argument about the "High Court of Parliament," a device designed to circumvent the requirement for a two-thirds majority to amend the entrenched clause of the Union Act.[4]

In 1951, the Nationalist Government wanted to remove the Coloured voters from the common roll in the Cape Province. The United Party objected, claiming that the bill required a two-thirds majority of a joint session of the two Houses of Parliament. The Speaker ruled against the United Party, the bill was passed by simple majorities, and the case of *Harris v. Dönges* was brought into the courts on United Party initiative. The Appelate Division of the Supreme Court, in a unanimous judgment, held that the entrenched clauses could indeed be amended

---

[4] The following account relies heavily on Carter, *op. cit.,* p. 119-144.

only by the two-thirds majority required constitutionally. The Government had claimed that the transfer of "sovereignty" from the British Parliament to the Union Parliament by the Statute of Westminster removed any restrictions on the Union Parliament. The Court disagreed, by analogy with the United States:

> It would be surprising to a constitutional lawyer to be told that that great and powerful country, the United States of America, is not a sovereign, independent country [commented Chief Justice Centlivres in the course of the judgment] simply because its Congress cannot pass any legislation which it pleases.[5]

As a result, the Separate Representation of Voters Bill was declared null and void. The Government countered by introducing the High Court of Parliament Bill, under which Parliament itself would become the final court of appeal. The Nationalists thereby tried to revive the old tradition of the English Parliament's acting primarily as a court, performing functions that we would now consider judicial rather than legislative. In Great Britain itself this tradition is retained in the Law Lords, the highest court of appeal, part of the House of Lords and therefore of Parliament. However, the British Parliament or the Law Lords has never, since the sixteenth century, acted to express the "will" of a contemporary majority against the judiciary and the accumulated majorities of all generations, past, present, and future.

The newly created High Court of Parliament met to reverse the Appeal Court's decision against the Separate Representation of Voters Act on August 28, 1952, but on the very next day the Cape court found the High Court of Parliament Act unconstitutional, and this judgment was unanimously upheld by the Appeal Court in November 1952. In 1953, Dr. Malan, the Prime Minister, tried to achieve the same end by following the constitutional procedure for amending the entrenched clause, but failed to muster the required majority. When he was succeeded by Mr. Strijdom, the new Prime Minister started by "packing" the Appelate Division of the Court, in a move reminiscent of President Franklin Roosevelt's project to pack the Supreme Court. More important, he had the Act of Union amended so as almost to double the size of the Senate, from 48 to 89 members, in such a way that the Nationalists held 77 seats against 30 previously. In February 1956, finally, a joint session of the two Houses passed the Union of South Africa Amendment Bill, by a vote of 173 to 68, that is, a clear two-thirds amending majority. When this was appealed to the Cape Supreme Court, its validity was upheld by a vote of ten to one. Coloured voters

[5] *Ibid.,* p. 128.

were taken off the common roll in the Cape Province. Subsequent events were to prove the correctness of a statement made by the English-language *Rand Daily Mail of* Johannesburg in 1952: "The Coloured vote *and* membership in the Commonwealth are at stake in the clash with the courts." [6] Less than ten years later, South Africa had become a Republic and withdrawn its application for readmission to the Common-wealth, because the Prime Minister, Dr. Verwoerd, thought that the other Commonwealth Prime Ministers were bringing excessive pressure to bear upon him to revise South Africa's *apartheid* or segregation policy.

The legal basis for *apartheid* had been laid both before and during this constitutional controversy in a series of laws designed to reduce contact between the races to the minimum by prohibiting mixed marriages or illicit carnal intercourse between whites and Africans, by getting the entire population to register and be classified according to race, by enforcing rigid residential and educational segregation, by planning the establishment of a series of "Bantustans"—reserves to which Africans will be confined when not working for the white economy and on which they are supposed to get a certain measure of self-govern-ment—and by other measures.

Legalistic *versus* Violent Politics

The constitutional controversy over removal of the Coloured voters from the common roll illustrates the peculiarly legalistic style of South African politics. In all the former and present British territories in Southern, Central, and East Africa, people are constantly discussing the feasibility and limitations of constitution building. This is true especially of the multi-racial countries like Kenya and the Rhodesias. When some-one recommends a constitution with a bill of rights that would protect various racial groups in their enjoyment of specified rights, African politicians often point to the experience of the Cape Coloureds with their entrenched franchise to show that bills of rights need not be fool-proof. This criticism is correct, in that no written constitution by itself ever presents foolproof guarantees—as citizens of the United States, both colored and white, must know. Nevertheless, the remarkable feature of "disentrenchment" of Clause 35 of the South Africa Act was that the Nationalist Government took as long about it as it did, abided by contrary court decisions, took so much trouble to circumvent these decisions by means of novel constitutional devices, generally couched its arguments in constitutional-legal terms, and never once made

[6] Quoted by Carter, *op. cit.,* p. 133.

the attempt to use or abuse its majority position and its control of the means of organized force to impose the *volkswil* by extra-constitutional methods. The Nationalists displayed the same legalistic patience in the course of the long drawn-out "Treason Trial," in which scores of white and non-white opponents of *apartheid* were tried for treasonable violations of the Suppression of Communism Act of 1950, only to have the first indictment thrown out by the court and finally to have all the defendants acquitted. On the international plane, too, the Union always argued its case—whether about South-West Africa, discrimination against Indians, or the Sharpeville shootings—in a very legalistic fashion.

At the time of the constitutional controversy, there were perfectly pragmatic reasons for the Nationalists' apparent patience. Until 1958, their parliamentary majority was partly the result of what Americans would call "gerrymandering." It also took them longer than 1956 to put their own political supporters into nearly all the controlling positions of the civil, military, and police services of the Union Government. But even by 1960, when they had succeeded in taking over the "apparatus" of government, they were still regulating their Parliament and court systems with British procedures, somewhat watered down. Right after the Sharpeville shootings in March 1960, Union judges, including Afrikaner judges, issued writs of *habeas corpus* to individuals detained under emergency regulations. It was an Afrikaner judge who acquitted the defendants in the Treason Trial. Considering the ultimate objectives of the Nationalists (beyond proclamation of their Republic and withdrawal from the Commonwealth), considering the width of the ideological gulf between themselves and their most outspoken opponents, and considering the means of violence at the disposal of Nationalist Governments, this kind of respect for due process of law seems sufficiently remarkable to call for an explanation.

Among a number of reasons for this peculiar legalism, we shall focus on two: the role of lawyers trained in English Common Law, and the African threat to the Europeans' monopoly of legitimate politics. Approximately one in seven members of parliament is a lawyer, and there is not much difference in this respect between the National and United Parties. These men are trained and experienced in the procedures of the Common Law, which qualifies them superbly for the conduct of politics in a non-violent and relatively unideological manner.

The second main reason for the Afrikaners' legalism is more convincing. The four to one proportion of nonwhites to whites naturally leads both Afrikaners and English-speaking South Africans to believe that they must stick together or hang separately. This kind of cooperation is made fairly easy by only slight differences on substantive policy toward Africans, Coloureds, and Asians between the National and United

Parties. The whites are so afraid of violence from the nonwhites, that they go to unusual lengths to avoid the outbreak of violence among themselves. This may explain in part why the Nationalist Governments have been more meticulous in avoiding outright violations of the Constitution than, for example, American State governments have been in similar situations. However, in the Union as in the United States, there subsists a kind of ambivalence between legalism and violence. Leanings toward violence have a fairly straightforward background in the "frontier" era especially of the Boers, but also of the English-speaking South Africans, and in the Boer War which brought the Union into being. Moreover, the violence used continually to control the nonwhite population is bound to make those who wield it against Africans readier to use violence in intra-European relations than their counterparts in, say, Canada.

Canada is useful for comparison once more, because both Afrikaners and French Canadians of Quebec tend to be ideological in the approach to, if not in the contents of, their politics. But politicians of both groups have usually justified their policies by historical recrimination and religious doctrine. In the case of the Afrikaners, this tendency is further strengthened by the *predikants,* many of whom have held leading political positions, and by the presence of many academics among the Nationalist leadership. Some of these received their degrees from Continental European universities, e.g. Dr. Verwoerd, who received his training as a psychologist in Germany. Unlike English-speaking universities, Continental ones have traditionally encouraged excessive systematization of knowledge which, in turn, easily leads to "packaging" it in ideologies and, ultimately, to unrealistic reliance upon the capability of this "knowledge" and its possessors, academically trained intellectuals, to solve all of society's problems. As in Germany, so in South Africa, it is not at all unusual to find members of parliament who wrote doctoral dissertations on, say, the relevance of Immanuel Kant's philosophy to the South African racial situation. In this way, religious-cultural ideology is backed up by academic ideology. The main factors that make the Nationalists at all willing to compromise with their white antagonists are similar to those which encourage constitutional and parliamentary legalism: fear of the consequences from the other side of the color bar, and the availability of Common Lawyers, who are agents of compromise par excellence wherever they may be.

The Procedures of Parliament

The process of hammering out compromises between antagonistic European parties is carried on mainly in the Union House of Assembly at Cape Town. (South Africa's legislative capital is at Cape Town, the administrative capital at Pretoria, and the judicial capital at Bloemfontein.) This is a British parliament, clearly copied from the prototype at Westminster. It bears all the advantages and disadvantages of transplantation to an even slightly un-British soil and climate. The procedures which facilitate debate by bringing relevant information and opinion to bear upon the issue under discussion, promote resolution with dispatch. As in London, the Speaker, who presides over deliberations, conducts himself as the impartial umpire of the debates and is deferred to with great respect. Parliamentary disorders, like scuffles and fistfights, hardly ever occur, in contrast to Continental parliaments.

On the other hand, British parliamentary procedure forces a two-way approach to everything: always the Opposition has to be pitched against the Government, even when there may be no genuine, "natural" ground for disagreement. In the United Kingdom itself, this method has usually yielded good results (except while the Irish were still at Westminster), because of the ancient and, therefore, almost subconscious commitment to the rules of the game, the procedures of politics. No British Government, even if supported by a large majority in the House of Commons, would attempt to bring about the kind of constitutional changes that the Nationalists undertook in the 1950's and again in 1960 in founding the Republic—even if such constitutional changes were necessary in order to achieve a set of substantive policy goals, like nationalization of industry which, in Great Britain, can be attained without constitutional change. The Nationalists, by contrast, with the possible exception of the Common Lawyers among them, are not that deeply committed to observing the rules of procedure. They are more concerned with the substance of their programs and policies. The United Party, though many of its members of parliament are Afrikaners, is more concerned with the methods used to accomplish a particular policy goal, that is, with procedures. (This relative difference in outlook between the two major parties is one of the main themes of Professor Carter's *The Politics of Inequality*). In the British Parliament no such difference exists; at Westminster every topic of debate is formulated in the form of two alternatives—either/or, for-or-against. This structures deliberation and focusses the attention of the public upon issues that may play a role in the next general election. In Cape Town, on the contrary, the two-way formulation of issues results in a pure clash of wills. In both places, the Opposition knows that any bill introduced by the Government will be passed, because the Government is the Government by virtue of its parliamentary majority. In Cape Town, however, there lurks behind every circumstantial measure, behind almost every question of day-to-day policy, the ultimate question of the Constitution itself—what the French call the question of the regime.

Representation, Parties, and Franchise

The House of Assembly elected in 1958 consisted of 103 Nationalists, 53 members of the United Party, four European representatives of the Coloured voters, and three of the Natives. The National Party thus controlled 66 per cent of the seats, although it had received slightly less than half, and the United Party slightly more than half of the popular vote. The discrepancy between popular vote and parliamentary representation had increased over 1953, as a result of new redistricting that favored the Nationalists.

From the outsider's point of view, it is noteworthy that the differences are only slight between the older parties and the new Progressives party, organized in 1960 from among members of the United Party, Coloured representatives, and Native representatives (whose seats were later abolished). This is shown by the "Main Principles and Policies" of the Progressive Party:

1) The maintenance and extension of the values of Western Civilisation, the protection of fundamental human rights and the safeguarding of the dignity and worth of the human person, irrespective of race, colour or creed.

2) The assurance that no citizen of the Union of South Africa shall be debarred on grounds of race, religion, language or sex, from making the contribution to our national life of which he or she may be capable.

. . .

4) The maintenance inviolate of the Rule of Law.

. . .

6) The promotion of friendly relations with other nations, more particularly the members of the Commonwealth and those who share with us the heritage of Western Civilisation.

CONSTITUTION AND FRANCHISE PROPOSALS

The Party regards our present flexible, highly centralised Constitution as entirely unsuited to South Africa, whose inhabitants comprise a plural society consisting of several racial communities. A Constitution of this kind may work well enough in a homogeneous society such as that of Great Britain in which deep-rooted constitutional conventions operate: but in a plural society such as ours it enables any group which happens, for the time being, to command a Parliamentary majority to dominate and to exercise unchecked power over the others. This inevitably causes, among the subject communities, growing frustration and hostility which threaten the very existence of civilised society in South Africa.

Among the constitutional reforms proposed, the following are of special interest to us:

1. To establish conditions which will enable the peoples of South Africa to live as one nation in accordance with the values and concepts of Western Civilisation.

2. To enable suitably qualified citizens of a defined degree of civilisation belonging to any population group to participate in the government of the country, according to their ability to assume responsibility, through the holding of public office and through registration on a common electoral roll for election of the members of the House of Assembly, with special provision for the representation of persons not so qualified.

. . .

4. To decentralise legislative and executive power by devolving on the existing provinces . . . such powers and functions as need not be exercised by the central Parliament and Government in the interests of the peace, safety and welfare of the Union as a whole. . . .

5. To guarantee, by inclusion in the Constitution of an entrenched Bill of Rights, the fundamental human rights and liberties of the individual, such as freedom of religion, speech and association, equal protection of the laws, and also the equal status of the official languages.

6. To ensure the maintenance in South Africa of an independent and learned judiciary, impartial justice and rule of law.

After a long section on economic and labour policy, and short ones on the urban African and identification of citizens, the statement addresses itself to

THE SOCIAL, RESIDENTIAL AND AMENITY ASPECTS

The Party accepts that economic integration is an established and permanent fact. It regards this as being in the interests of all the people of this country. It recognises, however, the social conventions which have grown up in South Africa over a long period and respects the desire of individuals to reside among and associate with people of their own race. It will not, therefore, force residential or social integration upon anyone, but equally it will not deprive people of different races of their freedom of association.

· · ·

THE REPUBLIC

The Party believes that the interests of South Africa demand internal peace and external security, and that both would be gravely endangered by a republic such as envisaged by the Nationalist Government. . . .

The concluding sections deal with various aspects of Education Policy.[7]

Our detailed consideration of the platform of the Progressive Party is not meant to suggest that it will be able to form a Government in what is now the Republic of South Africa. Rather, its program is intended to highlight the difficulties of any "progressive" group of Europeans in that country, as well as the extent of agreement that prevails between even these Progressives and the two major parties. In terms of the latter consideration, the most interesting planks are those that show how reluctant the Progressives were to appear too radical. For instance, they explicitly state that they would not force residential integration upon anyone. Had they remained silent on this point, the other two parties—not the Nationalists alone—would have accused them of favoring residential integration, and that would have finished any chances of attracting white voters, which were minimum in the first place. In the election of 1961, the Progressive Party won one seat.

Another index of the Progressives' "European conventionality," as we might call it, is their repeated appeal to the standards of "European Civilisation," especially in connection with qualifications for the franchise. Throughout British Southern, Central, and East Africa, the franchise has always been the most divisive issue, both among whites, and between them and nonwhites. Very few Europeans favor universal suffrage. For example, one South African member of parliament, who had belonged to the tiny Liberal Party which advances a fully egalitarian program, joined the Progressives precisely because he could no longer stomach the Liberals' espousal of universal franchise. Europeans oppose this because, they say, the Africans are not yet sufficiently "civilized" to understand the meaning of the vote. If the Africans were given "one man, one vote," the slogan of most independence movements, then the Europeans fear they would be swamped by the Africans and the country would be run by a "bunch of uncivilized, irresponsible, radical, dema-gogic, power hungry and self-seeking agitators."

We shall deal with these arguments in greater detail in discussing

[7] The Progressive Party of South Africa, *Main Principles and Policies Adopted at Inaugural Congress, November 13th & 14th, 1959, Johannesburg*, 6 pp.

the Federation of Rhodesia and Nyasaland, where they were elaborated to the highest degree. In the Federation as a whole and its three member Territories Africans did have the vote, based on four frequently changing different sets of property and educational qualifications. In the South African election of 1958, Cape Coloureds could vote on their separate roll, if they were literate and owned property worth £75 or earned £50 a year. Espousal by the South African Progressive Party of a highly qualified franchise, under which some of the now wholly disqualified Africans could qualify for the vote, illustrates what we might describe as a tragic law of European "liberalism" in Africa. The most liberal group of Europeans in each territory advocates measures for African advancement—especially in the franchise—that have already been put into effect in the next territory to the north where, in turn, the even more progressive policies already in effect in its next northern neighbor *should* have been put into operation a year or two earlier, *if* its African independence movement were to have been satisfied even in part.

What makes the situation in South Africa even more tragic is the hopelessness of Progressive or similar persuasion, because the Nationalist Government has been moving in the opposite direction. In the referendum on the republic issue of 1960, the Nationalists won a majority of the popular European vote for the first time, losing only in the predominantly English-speaking province of Natal. (This, incidentally, goes far toward explaining the Progressives' advocacy of decentralization along more federal, less unitary lines.) After this victory, Dr. Verwoerd, the Prime Minister, removed the New Republic of South Africa from the Commonwealth, precisely on the issue of *apartheid*. Thereafter, the Afrikaner Nationalists could without restraint put into effect the *volkswil*, which some of their leaders seemed to identify with the will of their God.

The Africans' Struggle: Peaceful or Violent?

So far we have left out of account the aspirations of the Africans, along with those of the Coloureds and Asians. Before establishment of the Republic, there was one focal point for these aspirations: the franchise. Leaders of nonwhite organizations concentrated upon the franchise in the belief that white politicians who were at least partly dependent upon non-European votes would become more responsive to their demands. Offhand this seems reasonable. However, every time demographic changes threatened to bring about a situation in which the nonwhite vote might have been decisive in elections the dominant whites raised the qualifications or averted this "threat" by other manipulations. This was true first in the old Cape Colony and later in the Union as a whole. To put it differently, historically the franchise has been the path of greatest resistance for the nonwhites. Their leaders might therefore be well advised to look for other roads. But what other roads are there? This raises questions about the political style of the unenfranchised population of the Republic of South Africa. Have they leaned toward violence and ideologism, or toward legalism and pragmatism?

South Africans and outside observers agree that the Africans of South Africa are more advanced culturally and economically than those of the British territories to the north. A relatively high proportion of these Africans has become a more or less permanent part of the industrial labor force. They have a higher standard of living than Africans who have stayed on the land. Since their higher level of information and education includes exposure to modern political notions and ideals (however misunderstood, or primitively understood, these may be), their aspirations are naturally also higher. Their relative well-being—a *very* relative matter in this case—should make for a potential revolutionary situation. After all, most revolutions were made, not by the starving and downtrodden masses, as Hollywood would have us believe, but by economically up-and-coming strata—like the French bourgeoisie, to take the classical case of the French Revolution—who were dissatisfied because their political advancement was lagging too far behind their economic progress. They resorted to violence. Is the same kind of development likely in South Africa?

There are two sides to this question, the internal and the external. To keep them distinct from one another will become increasingly difficult, as Africans in the Republic get more and more help from Africans outside it through the governments of the increasing number of self-governing African states. To the extent that these two aspects of the question can be kept separate, one hopeful factor lies in the public commitment to nonviolence of the oldest of black South African political movements, the African National Congress. Its leader, Chief Albert Luthuli, was awarded the Nobel Prize for Peace in 1961. The Pan-Africanist Congress, which split off from the ANC before the passbook boycott that led to the Sharpeville shootings of 1960, has been accused by the Government of favoring violence, but this charge has not been proved. African political leaders might be willing to use force mainly because of the Government's demonstrated readiness to resort to massive police violence for both punitive and deterrent purposes.

One African leader, when asked about the possibility of an effective general strike, ruled this out without so much as a second thought because, he said, the Afrikaner police would just mow down the strikers with machine guns. Another was asked about the feasibility of using passive resistance along the lines of Mahatma Gandhi, who first developed his doctrine of passive disobedience *(satyagraha)* on behalf of his fellow Indians of South Africa. The African replied that the Indians could succeed with this sort of practice against the British, because the British "after all, are reasonable people. If we tried to lie down across the railway tracks here in South Africa, the Afrikaners would run the trains right over our bodies." And so they well might. There are some African leaders who would like to precipitate such a violent clash, because they see themselves as the eventual victors and think that this kind of violence would forge greater unity among their people than existed in 1961. However, most African leaders, and even more Coloured and Asian leaders, convey the impression—and it cannot be anything more than an impression—that they prefer to fight by legal and constitutional means, even though they expect little result from this, at least for the time being. They are not likely to support tepid proposals for constitutional and franchise reform of the type put forward by the Progressive Party, simply because these do not go nearly far enough. Rather, as internal legal channels are closed off, or filled with obstacles for them, they will increasingly turn to the external counterparts of these channels. They will try to have their case put before the United Nations, the International Court, and other international bodies, both public and private, like worldwide religious organizations. They will try to have other western states, particularly the United Kingdom even after South Africa's departure from the Commonwealth, put pressure upon the Republic's Government to relax repression of the nonwhites. They will encourage foreign nongovernmental organizations like trade unions to apply economic pressures to South Africa, as in the case of the boycott of its exports by the British Trade Union Congress. Partly on their urging and partly on the initiative of independent African states, South African ships and planes were denied landing rights by countries like Ghana and Nigeria, in 1960. In 1961, the United Nations General Assembly urged member states to bring pressure to bear on the Republic to change its racial policy. Meanwhile, nonwhite leaders are turning more and more for indirect and direct help, including in the end perhaps weapons and troops, to the newly African-governed states to the north of them.

As to the final outcome of the South African drama there can be little doubt. The racial policy of the Nationalist Party will have to be thrown overboard. It is too much out of step with the trend in race relations and politics all over the globe, and global communications are so rapid and accurate nowadays that the drift both of this trend and of South Africa's reactionary countercurrent are publicized too widely for continuance. If the whites of South Africa are lucky, they may achieve a genuinely "multi-racial" political system, or a division into European-

governed enclaves surrounded by African-governed territories, like
Basutoland (to which we turn next) in reverse—"only more so." If they
are unlucky—and the Afrikaners will have only themselves to blame—
those of them who have not been killed or driven out of their country
may become a disenfranchised minority, ruled by the vast African majority, enjoying as few or fewer rights than they had granted that majority
previously. *When* either of these eventualities will happen is a matter of
duration and, like most changes in Africa today, of not much duration.
Which one of them will happen, and how much violence will be used
in the course of it, depends basically upon the resolution that the die-
hards among the Afrikaners will be able to muster in support of their
ideologically dictated goals.

Western students of African politics often inquire, concerning independence movements, how much and what kind of force would have
kept a specific country from throwing out its European colonial rulers.
The question could be reworded to ask what France, Britain, Belgium,
or Portugal would have had to do to repress African "nationalism" and
prevent such events as the admission of a score of African states to
the United Nations? The answer is that this was not a matter of force,
but of resolution or commitment on the part of the Europeans. Any
metropolitan power totally committed to retaining control over its
colonies can do so with relatively little armed force. Portugal's "success"
until the uprising in Angola in 1961 is a case in point. But "total commitment" means the agreement with this policy of almost everyone:
colonial settlers, soldiers, missionaries, administrators, the metropolitan
government, and the masses of its population. Without this kind of total
commitment, marshalling even the greatest possible force could not
permanently suppress demands for independence.

The English-speaking whites, though many of them may tacitly favor
apartheid or similar policies, cannot be expected to make any real
sacrifices to insure its continued enforcement. Even the Afrikaners do not
have this total commitment. Starting about 1960, relatively liberal views
were voiced even from within the Dutch Reformed Church. After the
Sharpeville shooting, many Europeans in the big cities were in a state of
considerable panic—afraid, among other things, to leave families alone in
the residential suburbs while the men were at work in town. Before the
unsuccessful nonwhite general strike scheduled to coincide with Republic
celebrations at the end of May 1961, Europeans stocked up food supplies
in anticipation of a possible state of siege. After Dr. Verwoerd announced
the decision to leave the Commonwealth, prices on the Johannesburg
stock exchange tumbled, and in the following months a heavy flight
of capital took place, and emigration exceeded immigration to an extent

regarded with alarm by many South Africans. When the United States started to vote against the Union at the United Nations, first over the Sharpeville shootings, many previous supporters of the policy that led to this particular tragedy began to feel and voice their qualms. However, after the parliamentary election of 1961, the Minister of Bantu Administration and Development said: "We will die—each and every one of us, every son and daughter of South Africa—rather than give up our nationhood."

The severed bond with the Commonwealth and events at the United Nations serve to drive home to South Africa's white people the Republic's increasing isolation from the international community, and especially its white, western sector, with whose "Western Civilisation" they have always sought to identify themselves. Increasing awareness of this isolation may lead to more realistic appraisal of their situation. If this occurs soon enough, then the availability of British political procedures and of politicians trained in the Common Law, backed up by the strong underlying commitment of a large part of the white population to the rule of law, may yet make possible a not too violent transition to massive African participation in politics and, next, to African equality or dominance in shaping South Africa's future. If this happier of the two alternative courses is followed, we need not expect a great deal of organized violence to be started on African initiative. Under Afrikaner rule, the Africans are understandably afraid to use violence. They have no recent tradition of the use of organized force to attain their goals. If the Africans do achieve their current goals largely as a result of international pressures, brought to a focus at and by the United Nations, they will probably end up by being as strongly committed to the peaceful goals enshrined in its Charter, as the already self-governing African members of the United Nations are today.

The other alternative was prophesied by Professor Arthur Keppel-Jones in 1947, when he published a novel entitled *When Smuts Goes: A History of South Africa from 1952-2010, First Published in 2015.* Keppel-Jones *may* have been wrong only about his timing. What he calls "the Ox-Wagon Republic" was established only in 1965. In 1977, South African bombers attack United Nations forces, whereupon British and American troops, after a bloody war, conquer the Republic. A period of chaos follows in South Africa. The British Protectorates of Basutoland and Swaziland are granted responsible government in 1982 and 1990, respectively. They prosper under African governments, while poverty and pestilence rule the neighboring Republic, most of whose surviving whites have emigrated to South America. Keppel-Jones brings out the tragedy of one possible future for South Africa in the conclusion of the book:

It is doubtful if many have any clear understanding of what has happened. The thoughts of most are probably well represented by the remarks which John Dudd, a man of European descent, and perhaps sixty years of age, made to Dr. Matterhorn of the Swiss Red Cross.

"We have been very unlucky, doctor. We have always had troubles in our country. When I was a boy it was the Jingoes—you know they were unpatriotic people who never put South Africa first. But they left, and then everything ought to have been all right. We had a Republic and a good, firm government. Yet foreign countries didn't like us, they destroyed our gold mines and stirred up a rebellion. After that they invaded the country and we had to change our government.

"So we thought: perhaps it's for the best, a Native government may not be so bad. We shook hands with the Natives and Coloureds and we said 'You are South Africans too, let's all work together for our country.' But, doctor, those people started killing one another. That sort of government is no good. Now you hear people say 'Bult was right, the Kaffirs ought to be kept down.' But no one dares to say that openly.

"If only we had been left alone, we could have been a happy country, but we have always had interference from overseas. Foreigners ought to stay in their own countries and mind their own business—of course I don't mean you, doctor. All because of England and other foreign countries we have had poverty, rebellion, war, famine and plague. Nothing has been spared us. What have we done to deserve this? Why have we had to suffer this? Why?" [8]

[8] Arthur Keppel-Jones, *When Smuts Goes: A History of South Africa from 1952-2010, First Published in 2015* (Pietermaritzburg: Shuter & Shooter, 1947), p. 270. Quoted by permission of the author.

Chapter V

The British Protectorates:
Tradition and Transition

*In perusing the shorthand report of the great Pitso . . . which
in several points recalls the* agora, *or assembly of freemen described
in the Homeric poems . . . I was struck by the freedom and
intelligence with which the speakers delivered their views.*[1]
—Lord Bryce

African Traditions of Government

There were political systems in Africa, including South Africa,
before the arrival of European colonizers. Some of these had all the
attributes of what we would call "government": "centralized authority,
administrative machinery, and judicial institutions." Other African political systems did not have government in this sense.[2] Examples of both
types survive to this day, though never in their pure pre-colonial form,
since they have all been more or less under the influence of the controlling colonial administration. We must remember not only this
European influence, but also that nearly all accounts of traditional
systems are seen for us through European (or American) eyes. Although
non-African influence and reporting will always severely limit our ability
to grasp the institutions and procedures used by Africans when they
were still on their own, we can approach understanding them by looking

[1] *Impressions of South Africa,* pp. 424-25, cited in Basutoland Council, *Report on
Constitutional Reform and Chieftainship Affairs,* p. 25.
[2] The distinction is made by M. Fortes and E. E. Evans-Pritchard, eds., *African
Political Systems,* p. 5.

at those African politics that seem to have preserved their pre-colonial form most closely.

The High Commission Territories

The three High Commission Territories, or British Protectorates, in South Africa, are particularly suited for this kind of inquiry. Basutoland is the most populous of the three Territories which continue to be exempt from South African rule because they have remained under British protection and under administration by the British High Commissioner and Ambassador in the Republic of South Africa. Basutoland became a Protectorate in 1868; its present population runs to about 800,000 Africans and 2,000 Europeans. Bechuanaland became a Protectorate in 1885; its population today consists of approximately 300,000 Africans and 2,500 Europeans. Swaziland, which became a Protectorate in 1903, has about 200,000 Africans and 4,000 Europeans, of whom an unusually high proportion are Afrikaners.

Of the three, we will focus upon Basutoland because it has the largest population of the three, is the most centrally located—being totally surrounded by the Republic—and can for our purposes illustrate the importance of all three for the politics of South Africa. This importance is great, due mainly to the survival of these separate political entities under distinct British control. The High Commission Territories have, for example, often served as sanctuaries for political refugees from the Union. But this role is less significant than recent constitutional developments which demonstrate the inclination of the British Government to move dependent peoples slowly but surely toward self-government within the Commonwealth, and also the capacity of the Africans to take the British up on this without bringing about chaos. Constitutional advancement in this sense has progressed farthest in Basutoland. Most male Basutos work sometime in South Africa, and a large proportion of them are in the Republic at any one time. This fact by itself serves to spread among the Republic's African subjects ideas that the Nationalist Government considers subversive of its Bantu policy. Nationalist spokesmen occasionally assert that the High Commision Protectorates are just what they have in mind when they speak of Bantustans. However, the Nationalists are unlikely to continue making this point after Basutoland and, a little later, the other two have achieved a real measure of self-government, as they will very soon.

In addition to our interest in these territories as "original" African political systems and as factors in South African politics, we might consider them from a third point of view, as illustrations of the infinite variety of British constitutional forms. At this point, we should merely note this. Later, in discussing the former French colonies, we shall see how much Great Britain and France have differed in this respect, and we shall ask what the post-independence consequences of this major difference in colonial constitutional policy may be for Africa as a whole.

The Queen's Protection

In the period following their Great Trek, the Boers of the Orange Free State engaged in constant violent clashes, involving land and cattle raids, with the Basuto tribe. The Basutos had a great chief, Moshoeshoe (or Moshesh), at that time. He appealed to the British in the Cape Colony for protection, which was granted. This means that Basutoland owes its present independence from the Republic of South Africa to circumstances arising out of early British-Boer conflicts. This has not been entirely forgotten by any of the three parties involved, Basutos, Afrikaners, and British. The Basutos themselves remember especially that Moshesh requested British protection and was granted this in return for pledging allegiance to Queen Victoria. That Basutoland, like the other two South African Protectorates—and also like Barotseland and other parts of Northern Rhodesia, Nyasaland, and Buganda, with local variations—invited Her Majesty's interest, so to speak, still gives special privileges to these Protectorates.

Their status as Protectorates has affected the political style of the Basutos (and others), particularly the type of arguments they use to justify their stand on issues like relations with the United Kingdom and with the Republic (the Federation of Rhodesia and Nyasaland, or Uganda). They lean toward legalism, for example by quoting early treaties and requests for, and grants of, protection. This comes out in the historical introduction to the *Report* of the Constitutional Reform Committee of the Basutoland Council, which laid the groundwork for the Constitution that came into effect in 1960. The *Report* quotes a letter of Moshoeshoe of 1862:

> What I desire is this—that the Queen should send a man to live with me, who will be her ear and eye and also her hand to work with me in political matters. He will protect the Basuto and gradually teach them to hear magistrates while he is helping me in political matters. . . .
>
> The Queen rules my people only through me. The man whom I ask from the Queen to live with me will guide and direct me. . . . When the agent and I agree as to what is right I shall carry it out.
>
> I wish to govern my people by native law, by our own laws, but if the

Queen after this wishes to introduce other laws into my country, I would be willing, but I would wish such laws to be submitted to the Council of the Basuto; and when they are accepted by my Council, I will send the Queen [sic] and inform her that they have become law. . . .[3]

The same *Report* also quotes the Proclamation of 1868, under which the Governor of the Cape Colony and High Commissioner extended British protection:

Whereas with a view to the restoration of peace and the future maintenance of tranquillity and good government on the north-eastern border of the Colony of the Cape of Good Hope, Her Majesty the Queen has been graciously pleased to comply with the request made by Moshesh, the Paramount Chief, and other Headmen of the tribe of the Basutos that the said tribe may be admitted into the allegiance of Her Majesty. . . . Now therefore I do hereby proclaim and declare that from and after the publication hereof the said tribe of the Basutos shall be and shall be taken to be for all intents and purposes British subjects; and the Territory of the said tribe shall be taken to be British Territory. And I hereby require all Her Majesty's subjects in South Africa to take notice of this my Proclamation accordingly.[4]

Except for the initial period of the Protectorate, when it came under the jurisdiction of the Cape Colony, it has been administered by the High Commissioner to the Union who, until adoption of the Statute of Westminster in 1931, was identical with the British-appointed Governor General of the Union. The South Africa Act provided that Basutoland could be absorbed by the Union after consultation with the Basutos. Internally, rule by the Paramount Chief was continued, and an established custom of holding large public meetings to discuss public affairs was modernized and very slowly institutionalized. Lord Bryce, one of the most distinguished students of comparative modern government and best known as the author of *The American Commonwealth*, described one of these meetings in a passage from which we quoted at the beginning of this chapter:

Once a year the Commissioner meets the whole people, in their national assembly called the Pitso—the name is derived from their verb "to call." . . . The Paramount Chief presides, and debate is mainly conducted by the chiefs; but all freemen, gentle and simple, have a right to speak in it. There is no voting, only a declaration, by shouts, of the general feeling. Though the Paramount Chief has been usually the person who convokes

[3] Basutoland Council, *op. cit.*, p. 23.
[4] *Ibid.*, pp. 15-16.

it, a magnate lower in rank might always, like Achilles in the Iliad, have it summoned when a fitting occasion arose. And it was generally preceded by a consultation among the leading men. . . .

In . . . the great Pitso held in 1879 . . . [o]ne observed: "This is our parliament, though it is a very disorderly parliament, because we are all mixed up, young and old; and we cannot accept any measure without discussion." . . . And a fourth, wishing to excuse any vehement expression he might use, observed: "We have a proverb which says that a man who makes a mistake in a public assembly cannot be killed." In this proverb there is the germ of the English "privilege of Parliament." It is easy to gather from the whole proceedings of these Pitsos how much more popular government has been among the Basuto than it was among the Zulus or Matebele.[5]

In 1886, a British official proposed to the new Paramount Chief, Letsie I, that a formal Council be set up. Three years later, he received an involved reply:

By this letter I say now it is my duty to reply to your letter, which is a proclamation; I told you that I was unable to answer your letter, my being alone, that I will have to meet with my sons and my brothers and the men belonging to the country, those whose names you will find in this letter. . . .

The matter which I speak about is that I say that it is some time that I have been considering about a Council for the Basuto Nation and I have not yet found a nicer way in which it will be conducted, and also a nicer way in which it can be preserved.

To-day I say that I consent to this Council being in this country; and that the members of this council be elected by myself and the nation; this is my request.

Now Chief, I say that in this matter of the council, I find that this will be a work that will show well; that the hut tax of Basutoland will be of use to the country, because this council will be for the whole nation; it will be for the presentation of the whole of Basutoland. . . .[6]

(Letsie's full letter is about double the length of the quoted passage.) The Council, when established by Proclamation, could advise and criticize only. These arrangements were found fault with from time to time, particularly by an organization known as the Progressive Association. Between 1938 and 1955, a number of reforms were effected, one of the most important of which was the establishment of the Basuto National Treasury in 1946 as a result mainly of efforts by Sir Charles Arden Clarke. (Sir Charles later presided as Governor over the last years of the

[5] Lord Bryce, *loc. cit.*
[6] Basutoland Council, *op. cit.*, pp. 27-28.

colonial Gold Coast, before it became Ghana. Still later, he was a member of the "Monckton" Commission to Review the Constitution of Rhodesia and Nyasaland. In 1961, he served as adviser to a constitutional reform committee in Swaziland. His career illustrates the varied use to which the experience of colonial administrators can be put by the British Government.) Arden Clarke believed that "The best form of education in the art and practice of government is the exercise of financial responsibility."

In 1919, the Progressive Association had asked that half the membership of the Council be elected. But this was not actually brought about until 1960. However, beginning in 1950, District Councils, whose members were appointed by the British Resident Commissioner and elected by tax payers, indirectly elected 36 of 100 members of the Basutoland Council. The proceedings of this Council were again praised by outside observers in terms as glowing as, if somewhat less romantic than, those used by Lord Bryce. Beginning in 1955, new demands arose for creating a real legislative council. The British Secretary of State for Commonwealth Relations indicated that he was willing to consider concrete recommendations. A Basuto committee was set up for the purpose of working out a set of recommendations. This committee was advised by Professor D. V. Cowen, of the Faculty of Law of Cape Town University, who had earlier won the case of *Harris v. Dönges* against the Nationalist Government. The committee's proposals were discussed at a conference held in London in late 1958, resulting in an Order in Council (the equivalent of an "executive order" in the United States) issued in September 1959. The new Basutoland National Council was inaugurated in March 1960, shortly after the British Trade Union Congress had begun its boycott of South African goods, and shortly before the shootings at Sharpeville.

The Queen's Withdrawal

Under the new Constitution, the Basutoland National Council had withheld from its jurisdiction the following matters: external affairs, defense, internal security, currency, public loans, customs and excise, posts and telegraphs, and the public service. The most important of these evidently involve relations with the Union, by which this British Protectorate is surrounded. This fact has given leaders of the Basutoland independence movement a peculiar ambivalence of a kind that we shall also encounter in Northern Rhodesia and Nyasaland. For their own constitutional advancement, they have to negotiate and bargain with the British Government, but vis-à-vis their most feared adversary—South Africa for Basuto, the Federation for the other two—"H.M.G.", as Her

Majesty's Government is usually referred to, continues to afford them real "protection." As a result, while they threaten and cajole the British into accelerating their internal constitutional progress, they are also afraid of withdrawal of external British protection before the internal "white settler" antagonist has been rendered harmless.

The Basutoland National Council of 1961 consisted of 80 members: 22 ex-officio principal chiefs, 14 nominees of the Paramount Chief, 4 British officials (Government Secretary, Financial Secretary, Legal Secretary, Commissioner of Local Government), and 40 elected members. The Executive Council (the equivalent of a cabinet) consists of the four officials, three members elected by the National Council, and one nominee of the Paramount Chief selected from the National Council. The District Councils consist in the main of elected members who, in turn, elect 40 to the National Council. In District Council elections, everyone over twenty-one years of age who had paid his tax and had been "lawfully present" for six months prior to registration was eligible to vote. The latter provision was designed to qualify an estimated 43 per cent who were "commuting" to the Union to work. They could cast their votes by proxy, and about 12 per cent of the 35,000 voters (out of 190,000 registered) did so in Basutoland's first "nation-wide" modern election.

The Executive Council was advisory to both the High Commissioner, who is represented locally by the Resident Commissioner, and the Paramount Chief. A College of Chiefs was also brought into being. The British Government retained the usual powers of reservation (delaying approval of a bill) and disallowance (veto). Its officials, including the High Commissioner, are under the control of the British Commonwealth Relations Office, though as civil servants they are members of the Colonial Service, which is normally controlled by the Colonial Office. This is of interest in view of proposals that have repeatedly been made in the United Kingdom to abolish the Colonial Office and Service and to transfer remnants of the latter to the Commonwealth Relations Office, especially after the shrinkage of Britain's colonies that took place in 1960, when Nigeria, the most populous remaining colony, achieved independence and full membership in the Commonwealth.

One unusual aspect of the Constitution of 1960 was the inclusion of chiefs, i.e., traditional authorities, in a unicameral legislative council, where they would have to get along with elected politicians who are presumably ill-disposed toward them. This presumption of ill feelings between elected and traditional authorities is made by Europeans all over Africa, though the facts do not always confirm it, as we shall see. British administrators on the spot, as well as Professor Cowen, regarded this arrangement as unique, though the British Secretary of State for the Colonies at the time of the simultaneous inauguration of the new

Constitution and the young new Paramount Chief compared it with somewhat older arrangements in Sierra Leone. Mr. Macleod who, at that time, was accused of wanting to liquidate remnants of the British Empire and, therefore, his own job, seemed willing to adapt, and experiment with, constitutional arrangements previously tried in other colonies, as he was negotiating in London with independence leaders from more than a score of colonies. British constitution-builders on the spot, however, tended to be completely problem-oriented and rather parochial, in Basutoland as elsewhere; even though they could draw upon the experience of many other present or former British territories, most of which had passed through more or less similar stages of constitutional development, and some of which had faced very similar problems on their road toward full independence. The marked contrast on this score with the French will become evident later.

Chiefs and Churches, Progressives and Politicians

Basutoland's most difficult problems were economic development and relations with the Republic. These two sets of problems overlap to a large extent, because the country has not been self-supporting. Since Basutoland itself has practically no industry of any kind, many of its able-bodied males are always away at work in South and South West Africa, and even the Rhodesias. Trade has been in the hands of Europeans and Asians, who were first asked to come in by Moshesh himself. Agricultural techniques are primitive and have contributed to a tremendous erosion problem. There were no hardtop roads in 1960, dirt roads were generally bad, and one got around best by Basuto pony.

However, merely because the most serious *problems* are economic ones, as elsewhere in Africa, these did not give rise to the hottest political *issues*. This happened only indirectly, for example, when the Agriculture Department used to spend most of its time and energy policing erosion control and was opposed in these efforts by the Basuto Congress Party, the local independence movement. The BCP was following a common pattern by singling out an issue related to land use for the mobilization of popular support. Conservation measures always tend to interfere with established customs and traditions, in which the peasant population least wants and understands disturbance. Independence movements all over Africa have realized this and increased their support and membership by opposing such interference, at least until they came into office. In Basutoland, parallel to political change, the Agriculture Department changed its anti-erosion activities from police to demonstrator work, which turned out to be much more successful.

In the election of the Council of 1960, the Basuto National Congress won 29 of the 40 elective seats, the "Elephant Party" won five, the National Party one, and independents five. The Paramount Chief added nine more independents, two National Party members, and three Progressives—members of the group that began to promote constitutional reform in 1919. These Progressives seemed to be suffering a fate often in store for the first advocates of African political advancement, who usually come from what, in terms of conventional European categories, would be described as an incipient middle class. By the time the reforms actually are carried out, they are cashed in on by the current "radicals," who may then even condemn their by now elderly forerunners as "stooges of colonialism." The older people in turn denounced the current Congress Party as violent revolutionaries or even as communists.

After the first campaign, the National Party accused Congress of election fraud in one district, but the Basutoland High Court threw out the suit. Some opponents of Congress assert that it plans to abolish the chieftainship in general, and particularly the position of Paramount Chief, which had fallen into some disrepute during the reign of a female regent, while the present Paramount Chief was being educated in England, where he last studied anthropology at Oxford University. His inauguration led to hopes that his traditional office would be strengthened sufficiently to provide a stable center from which increasing political participation could be extended. The new Paramount Chief was undoubtedly one of the best educated Basutos of his generation, which suggests, incidentally, that the presumed conflict between "traditional" and "modern" political elites is more complicated than simple juxtaposition of these two labels would lead us to believe. Leaders of the Congress Party denied that they planned to abolish the chieftainship, saying that they only wished to eliminate certain abuses, like inequitable land allotments by chiefs, requirement for excessive work, or the alleged levying of fines on men who failed to attend the new Paramount Chief's inauguration in March 1960.

During their election campaign, the Congress Party mobilized anti-white sentiments. When one of its leaders was asked whether there were no good Europeans in Basutoland, if only missionaries, he replied, "Perhaps there have been some good ones, but I don't know of any."

This campaign in Basutoland was also complicated by charges of church interference in politics. The Congress accused the Roman Catholic Church of openly supporting National Party candidates. Similar charges were made by Congress' counterparts in Nyasaland and Uganda against allegedly Roman Catholic political parties in those territories. The leaders of Congress resent the paternalistic attitudes of some missionaries, in this case particularly Roman Catholics. In some other territories,

Catholic missionaries have collaborated closely with independence politicians, who have there opposed missionaries from other Christian denominations. Their resentment of the Catholic hierarchy in Basutoland is remarkable in view of the location of Pius XII University College in Roma, near the administrative capital of Maseru. This college has trained African independence leaders from all over Southern, Central, and East Africa. One explanation may lie in the long years of service that most of the missionaries have put in, so that the older ones among them have difficulty adjusting to the close of the era of paternalism, even in relations between teacher and taught.

Congress leaders were aware of the "objective" primacy of the overlapping economic and external problems of their country, but—as everywhere in Africa—they denied that there were economic solutions to this situation. They wanted to make Basutoland as nearly self-sufficient as possible, by developing local industries. And they believed that they would be able to accomplish this only after attainment of true self-government. Once this goal had been reached, they said, they would prefer to industrialize with help from the United Nations and the United States rather than from Great Britain, again betraying the peculiar ambivalent attitude of "British Protected Persons" toward their Protectors.

These leaders had been in direct contact with the Pan-African Freedom Movement and were in receipt of financial aid from it. As a result, unlike other independence movements at a parallel stage of development, they were little worried by problems of party finance. For example, they had enough money to pay for internal and foreign transportation. Instead, their main worry was interference, and eventually actual invasion, from the Republic of South Africa. They used a phrase that one hears frequently in Southern Africa: "Things will get worse before they get better." Things will get better when Africans all over Southern Africa get their freedom. They will get worse first, because Basutoland is militarily and economically indefensible. These leaders, because their country is an enclave within the Republic, are virtually forced to think and speak in terms involving military violence. Nevertheless, when they speak of their relations with the British, they continue to do so in very legalistic terms.

Participation by the Basuto Congress Party in both the Basutoland National Council and the new Executive Council, and the experience with British political procedures that they will gain on these bodies, may eventually enable the Basutos to make a positive contribution to solving the constitutional problems of their giant neighbor, within whose sea of coercion and discrimination Basutoland stands like an island of freedom and equality. Perhaps we can draw similar hope from the assessment of the Basutoland Council of 1910, made by the then Government Secretary, a British Colonial servant:

> Proceedings are formal and regular, and indiscriminate argument is not allowed. The point that would probably strike a visitor would be the courtesy and politeness with which members treat each other, as well as the moderate tone of the speeches made in the course of debate. It would seem that nervousness is a product of civilisation, for in this Council whose members have only comparatively lately come into contact with European forms of procedure, every member speaks fluently and easily and it is practically unknown for a speaker to stammer, hesitate, or repeat himself unconsciously. The principal fault to be found with the debates is their tendency to drag on to undue lengths, and as a result it has been found that there is always business left unfinished at the close of the session.[7]

The last comment on the drawn-out character of the debates could have been stated in a positive fashion, to point to the capacity, noted earlier, for almost infinite deliberation of many Africans in their own traditional political systems, in order to arrive in the end at consensus on a compromise, no matter how irreconcilable their several positions may have seemed to outsiders at the beginning of the debates.

British Protectorates *versus* Afrikaner Republic

Bechuanaland should be mentioned in connection with this optimistic estimate of the deliberative capacity of many Africans, which is rooted in their own political traditions and sometimes buttressed by the adoption and adaptation of British procedures. In 1948, Seretse Khama, Chief-designate of the Bamangwato, who was a student at Balliol College, Oxford, married a British girl. His uncle, Tshekedi, regent since 1926, was opposed to this mixed marriage. As a result, a split developed in the tribe, which was not healed until Seretse's return home in 1956. By this time, the British Government had given up all hope of restoring the chieftainship to its former stature, and began instead to develop a system of councils within the tribe. But in 1961, the general reconciliation had proceeded so far, that Seretse Khama was made a member of the Order of the British Empire and, more important, became one of two African members of the Bechuanaland Executive Council. This illustrates not only that here again Africans were able over a period of years to overcome deep differences among themselves, but also that the metropolitan

[7] *Ibid.*, pp. 45-46.

government could not sustain a policy in any way based upon the discriminations of color bar.

Even more important is the fact that all this occurred in a British Protectorate inside the Union of South Africa, which was at the time moving toward full implementation of *apartheid*. At the same time, too, the Federation of Rhodesia and Nyasaland was being founded on the borders of both Bechuanaland and the Union. The Federation was constitutionally dedicated to a policy of multi-racial partnership, whatever other motives some of its founders may have been trying to hide behind the façade of that slogan. By these means the British Government, which was the most important of the four governments that together founded the Federation, sought to drive home to the Afrikaner Nationalists how very much out of step they were with the rest of the world. That the Afrikaners knew this, but kept right on moving in the same direction, is the cause of the tragedy in the recent history of South Africa.

Chapter VI

The Rhodesias and Nyasaland:
Partnership and Federation

*The Government is placed and remains in the hands of civilized
and responsible persons.*[1]
—Report of the Franchise Commission

Motivation and Realization

We move from the realm of tragedy to that of quasi-comedy as
we cross the Limpopo River northward from South Africa to the
Federation of Rhodesia and Nyasaland. The leading characters of the
Federation have their limitations, comic and otherwise, but only a few
have politically relevant passions. At least in comparison with the Republic, a happy ending also seems to be in store for the vast masses of
supporting actors—if not for all the leads—in the historical drama performed in the two Rhodesias and Nyasaland. The happiness of endings
is, of course, a relative matter: relative to comparable stories elsewhere,
to real or avowed motives of the actors, or to the best possible ending
that the observer could reasonably have expected. Many observers and
some participants have already adjudged the Federation a failure by
all of these standards but the first, comparison with its neighbor to the
south. Can we agree with these judgments?

The Federation of Rhodesia and Nyasaland was brought into being,
in 1953, partly in response to the course that events had been given

[1] From the "Terms of Reference," Government of Southern Rhodesia, Franchise
Commission (Tredgold Commission), *Report,* 1957.

77

by the National Party in the Union, south of the Limpopo River. In the Preamble to the Constitution of the Federation, issued as an Order in Council, the British Government gave notice to the Union Government, among others, that it intended to retain authority over the "political advancement of the peoples" of Northern Rhodesia and Nyasaland, and that the new Federation "would foster [multi-racial] partnership and co-operation between their inhabitants." As we have seen, none of these signals deterred the South Africans from their charted course.

Let us therefore examine the real and the avowed motives of the early proponents and opponents of federation between Southern Rhodesia, Northern Rhodesia, and Nyasaland. We can read the avowed motives on the constitutional record: Southern Rhodesia, a self-governing Colony since 1923, was to continue "to enjoy responsible government in accordance with its constitution." Northern Rhodesia and Nyasaland "should continue, under the special protection of Her Majesty, to enjoy separate Governments for so long as their respective peoples so desire." And

> the association of the Colony and territories aforesaid in a Federation under Her Majesty's sovereignty, enjoying responsible government in accordance with this Constitution, would conduce to the security, advancement and welfare of all their inhabitants, and in particular would foster partnership and co-operation between their inhabitants and enable the Federation, when those inhabitants so desire, to go forward with confidence towards the attainment of full membership of the Commonwealth.[2]

The Constitution provided for its own review by a conference consisting of delegations from the five governments involved—the British, the Federal, and the three territorial ones. When this conference first met, in December 1960, "strict constructionists" could have said that the Federation had more or less realized all but one of the avowed intentions of its founders. The one exception was advance toward full membership in the Commonwealth. There were, however, no strict constructionists is this sense among the participants in the conference. Instead, there were the leaders of the African independence movements in the three territories, all of them vehemently opposed to continuing the Federation. The white leaders of the Federal Government and, with somewhat less commitment, of the Southern Rhodesian Government, came out just as strongly in favor of a strengthened Federation which should then soon achieve "dominion status" in the Commonwealth. The British Government, for its part, based its attitude largely

---

[2] Preamble, *The Constitution of the Federation of Rhodesia and Nayasland.*

on the recommendations of the "Monckton Commission," an Advisory Commission on the Review of the Constitution of Rhodesia and Nyasaland. This Commission had recommended retention of the Federation with major constitutional reforms, including the return of many federal powers to the territorial governments; equal representation of blacks and whites in the Federal Parliament (instead of the prevailing 12:59 ratio); elimination of racial discrimination; and a right of secession for the two northern territories after their governments had become more broadly representative, i.e., after they had become African.

These recommendations indicate that the intentions of the founders of the Federation, published in the Preamble to its Constitution, had not been realized in the course of the seven years leading up to the review conference. The fact that this conference had to be adjourned without reaching any decisions suggests that the Federation had been a dismal failure. This conclusion could be supported further by the apparent failure of another simultaneous conference in London, this one on the Constitution of Northern Rhodesia, whose "incumbent" Constitution had been in operation for barely two years. At the same time, negotiations between white and black Southern Rhodesian leaders and the British Secretary of State for Commonwealth Relations about the constitutional advancement of Africans in the Colony for a time also threatened to break down.

If the avowed constitutional motives remained unsatisfied to such a large degree, perhaps the real motives of both proponents and opponents of Federation fared better. Both the Europeans in Southern Rhodesia, who made up less than one-tenth of its population, and the British wanted to strengthen the British connection in view of the anti-British policies of South African Governments after 1948. They also wanted to make the three territories economically more viable. Europeans in Southern Rhodesia, whose legislation was still subject to British disallowance if it discriminated against Natives, wanted to escape these restrictions. Europeans in Northern Rhodesia, where they made up only about three per cent of the population, wanted to get rid of British Colonial Office control of the government of their territory. The Colonial Office, which was also responsible for Nyasaland, wanted to improve the economy of Nyasaland, which was described as a "colonial slum" as recently as 1960, by Lord Home, who was then Secretary of State for Commonwealth Relations. The British Government wanted to bring about a public declaration by Southern Rhodesia of differences between its and South Africa's racial policies. Africans, on the other hand, especially in the northern territories, opposed the link with "white settler dominated" Southern Rhodesia, partly because they saw little difference between what it practiced and what the Afrikaners preached in their doctrine of *apartheid*. They were afraid that the Southern Rhodesian land policy, under which half of the arable land was reserved for Europeans, would be extended to Northern Rhodesia and Nyasaland where, under British Protection, nearly all land was held in trust for Africans. They also feared, in spite of the constitutional Preamble, that British protection would be replaced by Southern Rhodesian white domination, through the Federal Parliament; only one-fifth of whose members—elected on a highly restricted franchise— were to be Africans.

With these attitudes motivating the "partners" to the federal bargain, the resulting constitutional arrangements were bound to be a series of rather unwieldy compromises. Have the results, after nine years, lived up to the expectations and intentions of either advocates or opponents of Federation? The British connection was definitely strengthened, as shown by the fact that there was virtually no sentiment in Southern Rhodesia in favor of joining South Africa's exodus from the Commonwealth. The economies of the three territories, jointly and separately, have become more viable, although the distribution of economic benefits among them, and between Europeans and Africans, has been quite uneven, and although no connection between economic improvement and Federation can be proved. Southern Rhodesia, as a result of constitutional reforms approved in a referendum in 1961, did throw off almost all British control over its African policy, but only in return for great modifications in that policy, including repeal of the Land Apportionment Act and elimination of many facets of discrimination. Its formerly all-white Parliament of thirty members was expanded to sixty-five, fifteen of them Africans. Northern Rhodesia experienced some unrest in 1961, when about twenty Africans protesting against inadequate constitutional reforms were killed by security forces in a series of outbreaks. But early internal self-government for Northern Rhodesia was indicated, partly in response to the sweeping victory of Dr. Hastings Kamuzu Banda's Malawi Congress Party in neighboring Nyasaland's first election on a broadened franchise. More than 95 per cent of 110,000 registered voters (of a population of about 3,000,000) went to the polls in completely orderly fashion, and Malawi Congress Party received 99 per cent of all votes cast on the lower roll. Dr. Banda was appointed Minister of Natural Resources and was expected to become the first Prime Minister of Nyasaland before long. He entertained the same Governor who had sent him to prison in Southern Rhodesia two years earlier. Multi-racial partnership had been achieved to the extent that political, and sometimes even social, collaboration between the races had reached a scope that its most starry-eyed advocates before 1953 would have thought inconceivable then; even the anti-federal

Dominion Party, sometimes called "white supremacist," sought African supporters, ran Africans for the Federal Parliament, and had one African Member of Parliament in its federal caucus. African land in the Northern territories continued to enjoy the protection of the Colonial Office, and the British Government repeatedly reasserted its intention to let Northern Rhodesia and Nyasaland continue as Protectorates "for so long as their respective peoples so desire."

The real motives behind the early attitudes of participants in the founding of the Federation have not only been largely satisfied, according to this interpretation, but in addition to this, considerable "fringe benefits" have accrued to the leading actors. None of the Africans, for example, was known outside his country until 1953. By 1960, the names of Dr. Hastings K. Banda, Mr. Kenneth Kaunda, and Mr. Joshua Nkomo, the leaders of the independence movements in Nyasaland, Northern and Southern Rhodesia, had become household words in Great Britain. All three of them had made one or more visits to the United States, where they secured assurances of economic, technical, and educational aid from public and private sources. White Rhodesians, too, had gained greatly in international prominence as a result of their experience as leaders of the Federation. Of course, these leaders would deny that weakening of the Federation, or its eventual break-up, amounts to a happy ending. But if they compared their situation with that of Europeans in neighboring countries with more or less similar problems, like South Africa, Angola, the Congo, or Kenya, they might change their minds. And we, too, as outside observers, might conclude that the Federation that was created in 1953 came close to providing the best possible transition from white settler rule and Colonial Office protection to independence for British Central Africa, whether the founders of Federation actually intended to facilitate transition to that goal or not.

Great Britain and the White Settlers

By 1960, all political conflict in the three territories had been boiled down to one major issue: survival or death of the Federation. The seven intervening years had been relatively calm. Violence occurred on a large scale only in 1959, when sixty Africans were killed by the police and military during emergency operations involving the arrest of several hundred leaders of Dr. Banda's Nyasaland African Congress; and again in 1960 and 1961, when a smaller number of Southern Rhodesian Africans were killed in the course of riots in several cities, breaking the proud record of the Southern Rhodesian police not to have killed a single person during security operations since the great Matabele Rebellion of 1896. In the same year, one white woman was burned to death by a Northern Rhodesian mob.

When the constitutional review conference began in December 1960, most of the African independence leaders had been released from jail —where they had spent about a year on the average—or orders exiling them had been lifted. This and their participation in the various constitutional conferences, by invitation of the British Government acting as host, made the European residents of the Rhodesias, the "white settlers," unhappy and apparently even panicky. They claimed that the African leaders were radical and violent extremists who would threaten the internal security of the Federation. On more than one occasion, the Federal and Southern Rhodesian Governments mobilized white reserve troops. The African politicians for their part countered by denouncing these policies as military and police repression, including passage of a bill by the Southern Rhodesian Parliament that legalized the detention of individuals without charge or trial and that was designed to curb the alleged inclinations to violence of the major African political movement, the National Democratic Party. As a result of these developments, both Africans and Europeans made increasingly uncompromising statements about the Federation, Africans threatened immediate secession upon their achievement of internal self-government in the two northern territories, and white settlers in Southern Rhodesia talked darkly of mounting a "Boston Tea Party" of their own and "going it alone." Such statements have led outside observers to make gloomy predictions about the outcome of individual constitutional conferences and the general future of British Central Africa. These predictions have turned out to be wrong in the past. Are they likely to prove false in the future?

In trying to answer this question, we must always remember that crucial decisions about the future of the Federation will be made not in its three capital cities, Salisbury, Lusaka, and Zomba, nor by white or black Rhodesians. They will be made in London, certainly with contributions from Rhodesia and Nyasaland, but ultimately by the British Government. Her Majesty's Government will of course not make these decisions in a "sovereign" manner—no government nowadays does; hence the obsolescence of the concept of sovereignty even for European international relations. The British Government will be responding partly to demands voiced and pressures applied from a variety of sources, only a few of which are in Africa. Many of them come from the plane of world politics, as we saw earlier. Some of the loudest voices and strongest pressures come from inside the United Kingdom. White settlers often complain that decisions about their future are made 6,000 miles away from Rhodesia by people who "know little and care less" about conditions in Africa. These complaints are not without justification, the more so because the problems of Britain's remaining African possessions are considered peripheral to the mainstream of British politics, by both politicians and public. Relatively more Britons than Americans are informed and concerned about Central Africa, partly because almost 300,000 of their "kith and kin" have been living there; but this still amounts to an only small segment of the British public. Nevertheless, some of those interested in British Central Africa can speak for very influential groups, like the Church of Scotland, which has been heavily involved in Nyasaland ever since Dr. Livingstone's days. The British South Africa Company, usually called the "Chartered Company," is also listened to, because it owned and administered both Rhodesias under Royal Charters, until Southern Rhodesia's voters chose responsible government instead of joining the Union in the referendum of 1923, whereupon Northern Rhodesia was transferred from Company to Colonial Office control. Some directors of the Company and other Rhodesian public figures are also members of the House of Lords and make a point of taking part in its debates on the Federation. Several Labour Party Members of Parliament, including former Colonial Secretaries, have taken a continuing interest in the "liquidation of the Empire" in general, and political advancement for Africans in particular.

Even so, Britain's African problems are still considered only peripheral to the major domestic and foreign decisions that British politicians have to make. Government policies about the Federation—or Kenya— and alternative policies offered by the Labour and Liberal oppositions are not likely to win many votes in a British general election. This means that any British Government, regardless of its political backing, can take a fairly detached view of African events, relatively uninfluenced by special interests or the fickleness of public opinion. This fact ultimately benefits the independence movements and, therefore, further aggravates the white settlers' resentment about being sold out. In some cases they blame "opportunistic and ambitious ministers," who consider their temporary tenure in the Colonial or Commonwealth Relations Office a mere stepping stone toward the Foreign Office or even to Number 10 Downing Street, the Prime Minister's residence. When the British Cabinet makes vital decisions about the franchise of Nyasaland or the next constitutional reform for Northern Rhodesia, it is likely to give priority to considerations other than the interests or opinions of less than 300,000 Europeans among a total population of more than 8,000,000. Because the Europeans in the two Rhodesias are keenly aware of this, they have frequently threatened to "go it alone" by declaring Southern Rhodesia's independence from the Crown, much as the American Colonists did in 1776—hence talk of a "Boston Tea Party." The analogy with the American Revolution is, of course, quite false, among other reasons because of the wholly different ratio between settlers and indigenous population. But that the white settlers, not Africans, make this analogy should cast further doubts on the American image of the "African Revolution" of our time.

European Resolution

Occasional threats by white settlers "to go it alone" raise important questions about the resolution they could muster if presented with an opportunity to realize them. We have dealt with similar questions about the Europeans in South Africa and about colonial powers that withdrew from other African territories despite their possession of a monopoly of armed force. In the Federation, and especially in Southern Rhodesia, the problem is more complicated. Whereas in South Africa the resolution of the resident white population has been decisive so far, and in the former colonies the commitment of the metropolitan power, in the Rhodesias the outcome will depend upon the often apparently antagonistic attitudes of the white settlers and the British Government. The latter is determined to move the two northern territories toward self-government and to press for greater African participation in Southern Rhodesian government and politics. The Southern Rhodesian whites, however, at least *sound* equally determined to move very slowly in this direction and to retain as much control over the northern territories as possible. How can we gauge the resolution with which they would back up these policy declarations in a situation in which "the chips are down"?

Two methods are frequently used for this purpose in western countries: studies of elections and party systems, and surveys of attitudes and opinions. Both have been applied to the Rhodesian situation, where neither can provide a satisfactory answer to our question. We shall discuss them, however, before proceeding to other approaches.

Election Studies. The limitations of conventional electoral analysis when applied to a small electorate like that of Southern Rhodesia, or the whole Federation, seem self-evident. Between 1924 and 1954, the total electorate rose from 22,000 to 50,000, of whom an average of less than 70 per cent cast their votes.[3] In other words, thirty members of the Southern Rhodesian Legislative Assembly were elected by about as many voters as elect a single member of parliament in many British constituencies—not to speak of Congressional Districts in the United States. In a way, this small-scale European politics appears particularly

[3] Colin Leys, *European Politics in Southern Rhodesia*, p. 196.

attractive to statistically inclined political scientists, to whom Southern Rhodesia may almost look like a little laboratory.

However, this approach encounters other disadvantages. For instance, the use of categories like "rural" and "urban," lower, middle, or upper class make relatively little sense. In these small constituencies, MP's and their constituents generally know one another, whether they live in the country or in towns. European politics has an intensely personal quality about it and may, in this respect, resemble American politics in the mid-eighteenth century, when present-day quantitative methods were not applied for the simple reason that they would not have answered questions anyone considered important at that time. The use of "class" categories can also easily lead to distortions, because of the strong corporatist strand that runs through all European politics in Africa. We have already noticed this in South Africa, despite the frequent overlap of economic and cultural dividing lines. Usually there is greater cohesion and identification of interests between two persons belonging to the same church or language group, than between two individuals who belong to the same economic class but to different cultural groups. In the Rhodesias, this kind of vertical stratification of interest identification—as distinguished from class stratification along horizontal lines—is even more marked. People of different economic strata feel that they have more in common with one another than with others of the same economic class for a variety of reasons: language plus religion, as in the case of Afrikaners, Greeks, or Sephardic Jews; religion, as in the case of Roman Catholics, Jews, Jehovah's Witnesses and other Protestant denominations and sects; country of origin, as in the case of more or less recent immigrants from Northern Ireland or Ireland, Scotland, Wales, or particular counties of England, Natal, or the Cape Province, and so on.

Colin Leys himself, the author of this particular study, clearly recognizes the greatest obstacle to a straight class analysis in particular, and to a European-American type of electoral study in general: it is simply the exclusion of Africans—more than nine-tenths of the population, and by far the poorest—from politics. The greatest problem of Southern Rhodesia has always been the racial problem, under which all other problems, economic, constitutional, or external, were always subsumed. Until 1961, however, when British pressure brought about the inclusion of fifteen Africans in an enlarged Legislative Assembly of sixty, no political issues arising out of this racial problem were ever admitted to Southern Rhodesian politics. As a result, European politics dealt with relatively unimportant, even petty, issues. On the crucial issues arising out of the racial problem, the white voters were at one. Similarly, African nonvoters were found to be at one, when the National Democratic Party staged its own "mock referendum" against the constitutional reform, just prior to the official referendum of July 1961. The procedures of British parliamentary politics used by the Southern Rhodesian Parliament encouraged the formulation of issues, regardless whether any real disagreements existed within Parliament or without. These procedures also encourage magnification of the resulting divisions and of the feelings expressed about them. (Americans experienced something similar during the "Great Debate" of the presidential campaign of 1960.) In the Rhodesian and other British cases, this happens because parliamentary procedure calls for a "loyal" opposition. In the early days of the colonial legislative council, the "unofficial" members of the council, representing various interests in the community, provide this opposition by opposing the "officials," who were appointed by the Governor. This pattern persists in later stages, encouraged by the very physical structure of legislative council chambers and by the rules of procedure, the Standing Orders, which are always copied from the House of Commons at Westminster. The parliamentary opposition naturally tends to follow the example set by its predecessors, the "unofficials," by organizing electoral support among the voters. As a result, two "parties" come into being, whereby the political scientist may discover a "two-party system" (or a one-party system, Leys' description of Southern Rhodesia). But these systems are quite unlike their counterparts in Europe or America. In any case, the information compiled as a result of looking at Rhodesian politics in terms of these categories is not designed to provide adequate answers to the all-important question of the commitment of the white settlers to maintaining the *status quo* and resisting greater African participation in politics.

Attitude Surveys. Are attitude surveys better suited to this task? Thomas M. Franck assumes that they are in his study of the politics of the Federation. He asked a representative sample of Europeans questions like the following:

> The Federal Government has recently decided that Africans travelling first or second class on the Railways should have the same dining-car privileges as Europeans. Do you agree? [4]

He also asked questions calling for one of four alternative responses:

> Suppose the Federal Territorial Governments were today elected by a franchise which gave the Africans more votes than the Europeans; which,

[4] Thomas M. Franck, *Race and Nationalism: The Struggle for Power in Rhodesia-Nyasaland*, p. 237.

in your opinion, of the following consequences would be most likely to occur:

a) Africans would permit qualified Europeans to continue to be the principal force in government?

b) Africans would themselves take over the Government but would run the country efficiently?

c) Africans would themselves take over the Government but would run the country inefficiently?

d) Africans would themselves take over the Government, would run the country inefficiently and would discriminate against the Europeans? [5]

Respondents were classified and compared in terms of geography, age, sex, religion, origin, length of residence in central Africa, and social-economic status.[6] Apparently this approach yielded some significant correlations, but the validity of these might be questioned. To begin with, Franck faces the same difficulty as Leys, because social-economic status does not mean the same thing in Rhodesia as in Great Britain or the United States. This criticism could perhaps be answered by pointing to certain countertests made through using the other categories. But even if this should satisfy us, the very fact of conducting an attitude survey among the white settlers suggests the underlying assumption of the whole study that the real decisions about African advancement in the Federation will be made by Europeans in the Federation, and perhaps even by them alone.

The fallacy of this assumption has often been demonstrated north of the Limpopo River, most recently in the Congo. Before the Belgian Government unexpectedly decided to give independence to the Congo, similar opinion polls had been conducted among Belgians resident in Elisabethville, then the provincial capital of Katanga. These polls indicated that various categories of people would react in different ways to removal of aspects of segregation. All these surveys suddenly became obsolete when the Belgian Government decided to remove all vestiges of color bar some months before the final grant of independence. Moreover, it was discovered that the actual reactions of the white residents, once they were faced with these novel facts, were quite different from their earlier "opinions."

Undoubtedly, no British Government will be able to treat the Federation and its Europeans as Belgium did the Congo and its Europeans, who had enjoyed no more political rights than the Congolese under colonial administration. Nevertheless, this sudden irrelevance of similar attitude surveys in the Congo highlights one very important and much

[5] *Ibid.*, p. 241.
[6] *Ibid.*, p. 3.

overlooked aspect of all opinion polling. There is a vast difference between the opinions people hold and the "will," or the "cash actions," with which they are willing to "pay off" once the chips are down and they are forced to act or react. In the United States, pollsters are often aware of this distinction and the difficulties it raises, but here polling has been going on for longer than anywhere else and Americans are used to it; indeed, they expect it, respond eagerly to it, and are disappointed when not polled at some time and for some purpose. This is not true to the same extent in Europe, and even less in European colonies. With a little exaggeration, the contrast can be made by saying that Americans yearn for publicity, while Europeans yearn for privacy and even secrecy. Most white settlers polled in Rhodesia identify polling with snooping and are resentful of social scientists in general and American social scientists in particular, because they are even more suspicious of them than they are of the United States as a substitute colonial power. The more intelligent respondents to questionnaires might even realize that the more conservative their replies and the over-all results of a survey, the better will their own interests have been served.

For all these reasons, attitude surveys of this type can at best tell us something about differences in *opinions* held by people of different categories, as these happen to be classified. They do not tell us enough about the speed or direction of changes in racial or constitutional policy; about the reactions of the present or a future electorate to new proposals from its leaders; or about the extremes to which Europeans, driven by their resolution, may go in rejecting or accepting changes in race relations or in the constitution—changes imposed partly or wholly from outside the Federation.

The Colonial Refugee Complex

If neither election studies nor attitude surveys are reliable guides to the future, can we find some other more reliable approach? In searching for one, we must realize that politics does not start with opinions, but with the formulation of issues. In the Rhodesian case, this function is often handled by the British Government with respect to the most crucial problems, such as the extension of the territorial franchises and the decentralization, and possible dismantling, of the Federation. We want to know how likely the Europeans are to react with armed force in such crisis situations, and whether we may expect their resistance to African political advancement to become as doctrinaire as that of their southern neighbors, the Afrikaners.

Everything in the history of the Rhodesias and in the political style of the white settlers suggests that they are more likely to be legalistic than violent, pragmatic than ideological in such circumstances. Southern Rhodesia has no tradition of private violence comparable to that of the American West. It was first occupied, not by pioneering individuals, but by the police column of Cecil Rhodes' Chartered Company. This same "British South Africa Police" (as it is still called long after all links with South Africa have been severed) had not killed a single person in anger between 1896 and 1960, as already mentioned. No one has ever been lynched in the Colony, in contrast to states in the American South. Not only is this tradition of violence absent, but there is also a positive commitment to the rule of law on the part of the British residents of the Federation—a commitment even stronger than that of the English-speaking opponents of the Afrikaners in the Union in the years before establishment of the Republic. That the white settlers are reluctant to deviate from due process of law is illustrated by the symbolic resignation from office of the Federal Chief Justice in 1960, in protest against passage by the Southern Rhodesian Parliament of the Law and Order Bill mentioned above. In this respect, many of the white settlers are, or try to be, almost more British than their cousins "at home."

Roughly one-fifth of the Southern Rhodesian whites are of Afrikaner origin, and they have never wielded much influence in the Colony. The others, who either are, or identify themselves with the British, generally display the pragmatic parliamentary approach to politics. None of them has ever tried to construct a complete ideology to rationalize racial attitudes. One explanation for this may be their occupational background as businessmen, prospectors, or capitalistic farmers—all pragmatic professions. They or their parents or grandparents did not come to the Rhodesias in order to act out or create a total ideology. They are therefore not likely to want to die for any such abstract system of thought.

It is questionable whether these settlers would be willing to die in defense of their material possessions—their land, their mines, their comfortable and even luxurious way of life. The fact that many of the present white settlers are refugees from other former European colonies points in the other direction. Many of them came to the Rhodesias from India, where they may have been officers in the Indian Civil Service or Army; from the British Palestine Service; from Indonesia, after the Netherlands were forced to give up that colony; from the Union where, as Britons, they could not stomach the anti-British policies of the Nationalist Government. This background makes them keenly aware of such phenomena as the Mau Mau uprising in Kenya, and it leads them to exaggerate the shortcomings of independent African governments, like Ghana's or the Congo's. They do not really believe that "multi-racial partnership" can work, in the Federation or elsewhere, nor do they regard themselves as permanent inhabitants of the Rhodesias. In some ways, these refugees from ex-colonies resemble refugees from the Nazis and Communists in Europe who, having lost all their possessions and indeed everything but their lives once, wanted in their countries of refuge mainly to give their children something that could not be taken away from them, especially a good education. Many whites who settled in Rhodesia since World War II betray similar symptoms of the refugee complex, in its colonial variation. They do not behave like men and women who want to fight to the bitter end or to make a last stand, but rather like people who want to live with the comforts of the "colonial situation" to which they have been used as long as possible. Under sufficient pressure from the British Government, they would probably be willing to reach a compromise with the Africans by making concessions to them and, if that should fail, to try their luck in another country.

Against this optimistic estimate of the likelihood of restraint on the part of the European residents one could cite many extreme and violent sounding statements made by their leaders before and at every conference on African advancement, especially in connection with the reform of the franchise.

The Franchise: "Civilization and Responsibility"

In 1956, the Southern Rhodesian Government appointed the Tredgold Commission, named after Sir Robert Tredgold, the federal Chief Justice, its chairman, "to consider and report on a system for the just representation of the people of the Colony in its Legislative Assembly, under which the government is placed, and remains in the hands of civilized and responsible persons. . . ." [7] The recommendations of this Commission, after voters' qualifications had been raised and the voting method complicated, became the basis for electoral legislation under which the next Southern Rhodesian Legislative Assembly was elected. Their acceptance by the Government that had appointed the Commission led to the resignation, under pressure from his caucus, of its Prime Minister, Mr. Garfield Todd. These recommendations can, therefore, serve as an illustration of franchise reform as an issue in European politics.

The Commission recommended that voters be allowed to qualify for either the general or the special vote. The latter was designed for Africans with an annual income of £180. Some Africans might qualify for the general vote, on the basis of one of the following three sets of prerequisites:

[7] Government of Southern Rhodesia, *loc. cit.*

1) Income of £720 or property valued at £1,500
2) Income of £480 or property valued at £1,000 *plus* the completion of primary education to Standard VI
3) Income of £300 or property valued at £500 *plus* completion of four forms of secondary education.

Special votes were to count for no more than half of the votes cast by general voters in any one constituency, but both types would have been registered on a "single roll" and voted for the same candidate. This differed from the federal franchise law passed in 1958, which provided for separate general and special voters rolls, the first of which elected both European and African members of the Federal Parliament, while the latter elected only the African members (and in Southern Rhodesia one European member to represent African interests). For the federal special vote, the minimum qualification was an income of £120 per annum plus the completion of a two year course of secondary education. Electoral laws for the Federation and its three Territories are hard to unravel and understand even for the professional student of such matters. However, their main object as it must appear to the Africans is revealed most clearly by the statistics on voters' registration in Southern Rhodesia before the election of 1953. Almost 49,000 Europeans were enrolled, 594 Asians, 570 Coloureds, and 441 Africans. At that time the qualification consisted of an annual income of £240 or of £500-worth of real estate.[8] This had been raised by stages from an original £50 per year or £75 of real estate. To Africans, therefore, the change in franchise qualifications seemed designed to keep them from effective participation. Many Southern Rhodesian politicians openly admitted that this was indeed their aim. Others, including the Tredgold Commission, insisted that what mattered was not the voters' race or color, but the maintenance of government in the hands of civilized and responsible persons. The vast majority of Southern Rhodesians, both white and black, identified civilization and responsibility as exclusive attributes of the Europeans. Europeans, including the Tredgold Commission, generally thought of the franchise as a privilege awarded to individuals on the basis of certain merits, somewhat like merit badges for Boy Scouts.[9] They profess to expect disastrous consequences from the extension of the suffrage to uneducated and (presumably economically) irresponsible people. Since these European settlers often proclaim that they will go to almost any length to resist the expansion of the electorate in this direction, or

[8] Thomas M. Franck, *op. cit.*, pp. 181-2.
[9] This approach was carried to its theoretical extreme by the Capricorn Africa Society, a multi-racial organization in British East and Central Africa, that advocated multiple votes up to six per voter, "earned" on the basis of various qualifications.

the association of their Southern Rhodesian Government with Northern Rhodesian or Nyasaland Governments based on such a franchise, their reasoning about the franchise is of some interest.

If this reasoning is honest, it rests upon one fundamental and mistaken assumption. The "system of representation," i.e., the franchise, actually does not place a British type of government in the hands of anyone, civilized and responsible or otherwise. Government is in the hands of the Crown and *its* ministers, who are not directly elected as such, but rather as members of parliament. The system of representation that produces the election of members of parliament only gives those who have the franchise an opportunity to express their consent to, or dissent from, the Crown's actions. If the Southern Rhodesians had really been worried about keeping *government* in the hands of civilized and responsible persons, they could have insured this by other devices having little or nothing to do with the franchise; for example, special qualifications for ministers, of income, property, education, experience, residence, age, or an oath to uphold and defend the constitution, in which a bill of rights could have been included. However, the results of the various Rhodesian franchise laws indicate that this was not the main worry of the white settlers; in multi-racial territories such actions are ultimately judged only by their results and not by the proclaimed motives of their authors. The result has been to keep the number of potential African voters very low and, worse than this, to lead African politicians to advise their followers to refrain from registering under an obviously discriminatory election law.

Nevertheless, the Africans have continued to pursue the goal of "one man, one vote." In other words, they have let the Europeans set the categories of debate for them, even to the point of trying to prove that Africans are civilized and responsible. African politicians may have been making a mistake in this respect, because the vote has always been the path of greatest resistance in British territories with white minorities. But African preoccupation with widening the franchise is understandable, since the vote is one of the primary ingredients of democracy which they did not have but wanted to acquire.

Franchise Reform in Britain, France, and Their Colonies

Africans understandably look upon universal suffrage as the symbol of their equality with both the resident Europeans who already enjoy it, and with the self-governing countries all over the world, including both camps of the Cold War. The Africans also assume that "one man, one vote" is their best constitutional instrument for attaining the substantive goals about which they feel most strongly: an end to discrimination, improvement of living conditions, and modernization. They may be quite wrong in this view. For example, there are few if any cases on the historical record of underprivileged majorities that did obtain their substantive goals primarily as the result of a broadening of the franchise. On the contrary, the workers' movements of various European countries passed through either one or the other of two quite different sequences. Either a Bonaparte or Bismarck granted universal male suffrage as a gift from above, so that it was not accompanied by any real influence on policy for the newly enfranchised masses; or underprivileged groups gained their substantive aims—like better working conditions, higher wages, shorter hours, equal educational opportunities—through other types of organizational activity and were afterwards content to accept universal suffrage as the final outward symbol of their substantive equality. This was the sequence in the United Kingdom where universal and equal suffrage did not arrive until the Labour Party, largely an outgrowth of trade union organization, had been in office as a majority government after World War II. American Negroes, too, won many of their fights against discrimination through such activities as the National Association for the Advancement of Colored People, rather than through the right to vote, which is still denied to many of them in southern states.

One of the main causes of all the franchise troubles in the Federation and other British territories is precisely the fact that universal suffrage came so late to the United Kingdom itself. Many Britons, and especially colonial types, are not at all sure that "one man, one vote" is a good thing for the "Mother Country" even today. Indeed, many of them are quite sure that it is the cause of most of the troubles of the twentieth century. They often point with horror to the United States, where they profess to see the penultimate results of democracy based upon universal suffrage, ran amuck. On such views and "facts" both the white settlers and the British Colonial Office build their elaborate theories in opposition to a precipitate broadening of the franchise.

The French never bothered to defend a restricted franchise on similar grounds. They extended it earlier in their colonies than the British; as we shall see later, this did not interfere with their continued control of these colonies. The French may have sensed from their own history that overprivileged minorities can continue to enjoy their special prerogatives without necessarily keeping the underprivileged majority unenfranchised. In extending the franchise, both British and French thus followed in their colonies more or less the same patterns that they had passed through in their domestic political development. In France, the franchise was extended—and occasionally restricted again—by leaps and bounds, often as a gift from above and usually not in response to demands for its extension from below. In Britain, the franchise was extended very gradually, in almost exact response to the amount of pressure exerted by those pushing for its extension from below. In France, extensions in the nineteenth century frequently were not accompanied by a proportionate increase in the actual influence on policy for the newly enfranchised voters. In Britain, the vote always meant potential influence on policy without, however, placing "government" in the hands of the new voters. The history of colonial franchises has been a repetition, with some variations, of each metropolitan model.

Educated Africans were schooled in the history of whichever "mother country" played parent to their colony. Even if this had not been so, Africans would have conducted their independence movements by analogy with progressive movements in their metropolis, because colonial administrators and European settlers patterned themselves after conservative or reactionary politicians in the history of their homeland, and the Africans had to deal first with these colonial officials and white settlers. That few of these historical analogies between African countries today and Europe in the nineteenth century are valid is ignored by those who make them, whether white or black. In one respect this may be a salutary factor, because it may lead the white settlers of British background to give in to African demands for extension of the vote with as much sensitive responsiveness and as little violence as did the British upper classes to the British lower classes.[10]

[10] Reasoning by analogy with British history was used in the "Note for Monckton Commission" prepared by a white settler whose experience as such started in 1911, and who joined the United National Independence Party in 1961, Lt. Col. Sir Stewart Gore-Brown: "For myself I am firmly convinced that the question of granting a genuinely liberal franchise on a common roll must, at any cost, be faced. Such a franchise must be implemented without delay, and it must confer equal voting powers on equal terms on both races, without any disingenuous catches or strings. If it results in an African majority in the Legislature, no matter, and if it causes Southern Rhodesia to secede that too cannot be helped. . . .

"Anything short of this and any further delay seem to me to be desperately dangerous policies. I suggest that conditions to-day in Northern Rhodesia are not unlike those which prevailed in Britain in 1832. Then as now the conflict was between Privilege and the People, and failure to reach a successful conclusion would have meant revolution." Mimeographed, ShiwaNg'andu, Northern Rhodesia, March 8, 1960.

The Need for Consent

The Africans state, and often overstate, their demands for "one man, one vote" in anticipation of franchise concessions. They have frequently overstated their demands by seeming to threaten violence in case full universal suffrage were not granted by a certain deadline. Similarly, the European politicians have understated the degree of extension they were willing to contemplate. This kind of bargaining process has often led outside observers to predict the imminent outbreak of massive violence in the Rhodesias, Nyasaland, and British East African territories. These prophecies of doom have always turned out to be false, largely because all the local participants at least sensed that they were engaged in a bargaining process in the best tradition of British parliamentary politics between Government and Opposition.

In bargaining, the Europeans used a variety of delaying tactics. One of these consisted of a prolonged debate about the relative merits of the common roll, under which all voters are registered on one roll and vote for candidates representing geographically defined districts, and of the communal roll, under which different racial communities are registered on different voters' rolls that elect candidates to represent racially defined communities. In the Rhodesias, Europeans have generally favored the common roll. They have justified this preference by arguing that only the common roll will base party politics on "real issues" rather than on racial issues; and that members of parliament, regardless of their own color, will conduct themselves in terms of the interest of the whole country if they are dependent for election or re-election upon the votes of members of all racial communities. However, this argument, like the injunction to keep government in the hands of civilized and responsible persons, is again based on the fallacious belief that British-type parliaments themselves actually govern. It ignores the need to elicit the consent of all those groups within any political system whose active dissent could halt or hinder seriously its operation.

The necessary consent was recognized in the franchise introduced in Tanganyika, Britain's East African UN Trusteeship Territory, in order to facilitate its transition to self-government and independence. The Tanganyika election law contained one major innovation: each constituency elected, from a common roll of voters, three members of the Legislative Council, one African, one European, and one Asian or Arab. As a result, all but one of the elected members turned out to be candidates of the Tanganyika African National Union, under whose leader, Mr. Julius Nyerere, the Territory gained full independence and membership in the United Nations late in 1961. In the Federation, where African MP's were elected by overwhelmingly white constituencies, they were usually dubbed "stooges" by the independence parties. In Tanganyika, where Europeans were elected by overwhelmingly non-European constituencies, these white MP's were sometimes called stooges of TANU.

To avoid the label of stooge, British colonial electoral engineering devised a new scheme for the first popular election in Kenya in 1961. Each of the minority racial communities first held a communal primary election (which the Colonial Secretary called facetiously an "appallingly American institution"). Only candidates who received more than a certain minimum percentage in the primary poll could stand in the general election with its predominantly African electorate, to avoid the election of "excessively liberal" Europeans, whom other whites would then regard as stooges of the African independence movements. In fact, however, this label was in the end pinned upon the successful white candidates by Europeans opposed to African advancement, who accused the Colonial Secretary of deliberately setting the qualifying percentage too low.

Meanwhile, for as long as Great Britain or British people continue to exert any political influence in African territories, they may be expected to continue to devise complicated election systems. White settlers will continue to predict dire consequences for any country that includes "irresponsible and uncivilized" persons in its electorate. And they will point to instances of electoral corruption or violence, and to "one-party states," as proof of their prophecies. Despite such "proof," they will allow the expansion of their own African electorates rapidly enough to avoid the African violence that can easily be generated by lack of legitimate channels for the expression of protest and dissent. The Europeans may even realize that their own attitudes toward the Africans provided the single most important stimulus for the growth of independence movements; that their failure to back these proclaimed attitudes was the single most important factor in a relatively nonviolent transition from white settler rule to government based upon popular consent. Such a happy ending to the drama of politics in the Rhodesias and Nyasaland —in which the decade of the Federation has been only one act—will signal the beginning of larger associations of communities in Central and East Africa and perhaps beyond.

Chapter VII

East Africa:
Tribalism and Violence

*We can never learn to govern ourselves unless we are actually
governing, and making necessary mistakes in the process, and taking
the consequences.*[1]

—Uganda National Congress

The Bias against Self-Government

Until 1960, both writers and readers of literature on politics in
Africa showed a definite preoccupation with the multi-racial territories,
that is, the Union, the Federation, Kenya, and in North Africa, Algeria.
Their main interest centered on relations between whites and blacks in
these countries. When this focus began to change in the course of 1960,
it did not shift to relations among the new African states as much as
to their probable future role in the Cold War. In other words, race
relations continued as the major concern, but now at the international
level. So far, we, too, have dealt with these two aspects of African
politics, and not with either relations among the new states, or the
pattern of politics that is being developed within each of them.

This center of gravity in the literature has a simple explanation: the
books have been written by and for white people. Most of the very few
black people with enough education to write books about their own
politics were until recently engaged in the anti-colonial—and therefore

[1] Uganda National Congress, "Memorandum on Constitutional Developments, and
Reforms in the Government of Toro" (unpub. mimeo., n.d.), p. 5, quoted by David
E. Apter, *The Political Kingdom in Uganda: A Study in Bureaucratic Nationalism*,
p. 327.

97

at bottom anti-white—movement toward independence. Since its achievement, they have been too busy as politicians for serious reflection about
the future pattern of politics in their countries or on their Continent.
As a result, African politicians contribute little to the question about
the prospects for African politics. But it is important to shift the focus
from the multi-racial territories, because their present problems will
soon have been solved. In shifting attention, we must avoid the bias
against African self-government held by many Europeans, and some
Americans, whose experience has been mainly with the multi-racial
areas. On the basis of this experience, they often forecast that violence,

corruption, and inefficiency will be the outstanding characteristics of
politics in independent African states, and that tribalism will become the
main motive for political action. These forecasts were often based on
dramatic pre-independence experiences like the Mau Mau rebellion in
Kenya, Buganda separatism in Uganda, Masai traditionalism in Tanganyika and Kenya and, since the independence of the former Belgian
Congo, the disorders that occurred there. How valid are these forecasts
and this whole way of looking at the new African politics? In this
chapter, we shall try to begin answering this question in terms of
illustrations drawn from British East Africa.

Mau Mau

Of the seven major tribes in the Kenya Colony, the Kikuyu were generally considered the most vigorous by Europeans. They were also more directly affected than other tribes by the settlement of European farmers in the "White Highlands." In the early 1950's, a secret terrorist movement started among the Kikuyu. With benefit of hindsight, it now seems that the British Colonial Administration first treated Mau Mau too lightly, and later, doing a complete about-face, treated it too harshly. As a result, the movement prospered from repression and was able to identify itself with the much wider cause of Kenya "nationalism." The Administration directly contributed to this process by trying and convicting Jomo Kenyatta for managing Mau Mau. Kenyatta was probably the best educated Kenyan of his generation, having studied and lived in England for seventeen years. After his sentence of seven years had expired, and the Government still insisted on keeping him "rusticated," Kenyatta's immediate release, return to politics, and installation as first Chief Minister of Kenya became the one rallying point of agreement between otherwise hostile African parties. On the other hand, some inflexible white settlers, remembering the Mau Mau experience, charged that the Colonial Administration, by permitting Kenyatta to live closer to Nairobi and to receive visits from African politicians and the press, and then freeing him completely and receiving him in London, was preparing the way for greater violence and chaos than even that in the Congo.

The most unusual aspect of the Mau Mau movement was its atavism. Its members were initiated by means of a series of oaths which, according to some psychologists' testimony, had the effect of transforming their personalities. These oaths were administered in ceremonies alleged to be revivals of primitive Kikuyu rites. Sworn members of the movement had to be prepared to kill anyone and to observe absolute secrecy. Most of their victims were other Kikuyus. Mau Mau murdered more than 1,800 Africans and thirty-six white civilians, of whom only one had been killed by the time of Jomo Kenyatta's arrest. More than 11,000 Mau Mau terrorists were killed in the course of the huge military operation that the Government mounted against the movement.

Neither Kenyatta during his trial, nor other African politicians during the height of the movement, admitted any connection with Mau Mau as it was described by the Kenya Government. In effect, they denied that any such organization existed. On the other hand, all those who accepted the Government's description as accurate condemned Mau Mau. Even as pro-African a person as Father Trevor Huddleston referred to Mau Mau as "wholly evil." [2] Today, most politically conscious Kikuyus might agree that Mau Mau was a regressive movement and that its over-all effect was to retard Kenya's advance toward independence. This does not preclude Mau Mau's becoming a major ingredient of the unifying lore of the new state. If this should happen, then it will be at least in part the result of the Kenya Government's methods of detecting, interpreting, and stamping out Mau Mau. These methods identified most prominent Kikuyu politicians with the movement, so that it became difficult for them—and required great personal courage—to appear to be for self-government and against Mau Mau at the same time.

There were repercussions beyond Kenya's borders. Kenyatta was widely supported by anti-colonialists in Great Britain and the Commonwealth, and his release, finally ordered in 1961, had been urged upon the British Government by several Prime Ministers of colored members of the Commonwealth; white settlers in other African territories became unduly fearful of similar rebellions by their African populations; and other independence movements weighed the possibility of resorting to similar terrorism. This last was revealed by the official inquiry conducted into the Nyasaland Emergency of 1959, conducted by a British Commission headed by Mr. Justice Devlin. Speaking of the two most radical leaders of the Nyasaland African National Congress, the Commission reported:

> . . . A difference may be drawn between the sort of violence that Mr. Chipembere and Mr. Chisiza sponsored and the sort of plot with which they are credited. They are certainly intelligent men who must have known that they could not succeed in taking over the government of the country by assassinating the Governor and his Council. "That would have been tantamount to declaring war" as Mr. Chisiza pertinently observed, "You cannot kill a representative of the Queen and expect people in the United Kingdom to take the whole thing lying down. After all we had the example of Kenya before our very eyes." [3]

The Rhodesian Federal Government, on the other hand, was convinced that the Congress was planning to massacre the Governor, declared the Emergency for that reason, and arrested hundreds of Congress leaders in a roundup which led to the shooting of sixty Africans. The Devlin Commission's analysis of the meeting at which the massacre was supposed to have been plotted is not only immediately relevant to the administrative problem of detecting African subversion, but also tells us something about the "looseness" of African political procedures:

[2] Government of Kenya, *Historical Survey of the Origins and Growth of Mau Mau*, p. 162.
[3] Nyasaland Commission of Inquiry, *Report*, p. 86.

After the customary prayer the meeting in the bush on Sunday began with a resumption of the discussion on matters of finance and organisation which had been left unfinished on the Saturday morning. As to what was discussed and decided after that there is an acute conflict of evidence. It is common ground that the possibility of the Government's constitutional proposals being unsatisfactory and the possibility of Dr. Banda's arrest were both considered and that there was discussion of what should be done in either of those events; one set of witnesses said that what was decided was that there should be non-cooperation but that violence was not even mentioned; another set said that every form of violence was discussed from sabotage to murder. Most of the evidence on either side is of doubtful value. . . . There does not emerge from it . . . any full or coherent account of what was discussed and decided. On many topics it is probable that *no clear line was drawn between discussion and decision*. It is not suggested by anyone that any resolutions were put to the meeting.[4]

This type of African meeting can probably be understood best in the light of tribal traditions of lengthy deliberation that may not necessarily be intended to lead to definite action. In the West, on the contrary, the ultimate goal of this kind of discussion is resolution of the issues and clearly defined action through the application of force to specific targets by the sovereign state. At this particular meeting in the Nyasaland bush, and at many other more formal political meetings elsewhere in Africa south of the Sahara, the purpose rather seems to be the creation of a general consensus, which will not require any specified action involving the use of force. This, however, was not the understanding of white settlers or colonial officials in either Nyasaland or Kenya, when they were confronted with more or less organized African activity against themselves. They dealt with the presumed threat as most governments of modern states would have, by military and police force. As a result, they quelled the rebellions that may or may not have been in the making. But their reaction also had another unintended and more important consequence of making more Africans politically conscious and of uniting these Africans against the state's use of organized violence toward themselves and their fellows.

Forecasts of Violence, Corruption, and Inefficiency

In the Rhodesias and Kenya, white settlers have often used the experience of Mau Mau to predict the eruption of violence on a major scale within recently colonial territories. Instances of corruption and ineffi-

[4] *Ibid.*, p. 50. Italics supplied.

ciency of African civil servants or party officers are used to prophesy the
complete breakdown of government soon after the final "scuttling of
the ship of colonialism." These forecasts seem unwarranted by pre-
independence evidence and, at least for former British colonies, post-
independence developments. Outbreaks of organized violence were at
least stimulated by—if they did not happen purely out of reaction to—
European initiative, in circumstances that denied to Africans legitimate
channels for registering their grievances. On the other hand, there have
been indications that, whenever such channels are opened up, many
Africans become much more cooperative toward the government. In
Basutoland, for instance, the switch of the Department of Agriculture
from policing conservation rules to using demonstrator farmers had this
result. European agriculture officers in East African territories, too, expected to get much better cooperation from African farmers once it was
known that the agriculture officers were working for an African government, responsive to the needs and feelings of the Africans themselves.

In any case, whether or not self-government will result in more co-
operation, violent events that occurred under colonial administration cannot logically be used to predict behavior after the attainment of self-
government. The major irritant is colonial government itself, and with
its removal, the "colonial situation," as Mannoni has called it, disappears.[5]
The colonial situation is characterized by the "natives'" feeling of
utter dependence upon the white colonizers. The colonizers give opportunities at least to some of the natives to become "autonomous"
individuals like the Europeans themselves. Natives who take advantage
of these opportunities find themselves in a very ambivalent position
between the two societies, while the rest of the population is made to
feel less secure than before colonisation. These feelings of dependence,
ambivalence, and insecurity result in sporadic and unplanned outbreaks
of violence against the colonizers who, in turn, are driven to exaggerate
the violence that has actually occurred, as well as their own violent
response to it. This exaggeration is a function of the psychology of
those who feel the "colonial vocation" and therefore have become
colonizers or white settlers. According to Mannoni, these men try to
re-enact their infantile phantasies of the type known to us from literature
through Defoe's *Robinson Crusoe* and Shakespeare's *The Tempest*. A
strong inferiority complex was among the motives that led them to
leave Europe and come to live in the colonies. We need not accept
Mannoni's psychological analysis to recognize, at this point in our
inquiry, that the removal of the colonial situation in truly independent
African states will make for a radical qualitative change in both causes

[5] O. Mannoni, *Prospero and Caliban: The Psychology of Colonisation, passim.*

and manifestations of political violence. That is why Mau Mau and its like cannot serve as sound guides to the future.

This still leaves the questions of corruption and inefficiency. It does not behoove Americans to criticize citizens of other countries with respect to corruption in government, so long as it remains doubtful whether any of them will match the massive scale on which it has been practiced in the United States at various times. The American example also suggests that a certain level of corruption, *if* practiced and detected during the formative stage of the political system, can have beneficial effects, by discouraging excessive deference to civil servants and by encouraging the public to be forever watchful of its servants in offices high and low. In another respect, we have to remember that what is interpreted as corruption by Europeans may also be nothing but another aspect of the colonial situation. In most multi-racial territories, whites received on the average about ten times as much pay for performing the same work as blacks. Their standard of living was roughly ten times higher. A European civil servant could afford to overlook a shilling, and even a pound, which he might have stolen out of the office cash box. For him, the question of honesty might arise only in connection with the award of a contract for £100,000. But for the African, one pound was the equivalent of a week's salary *and* he might feel that he was taking it from an entity, the Government, which was doing no good for either his people or himself.

As for the acceptance of "bribes" by African civil servants and politicians, we have to remember that these gifts are made and accepted by people who may not yet have moved fully into a money economy. Moreover, these practices are often continuations of old tribal customs of exchanging presents, in societies that may have had poorly developed notions of "private" property. Where African judges appear to accept bribes from parties to a suit, we should remember that we pay court and lawyers' fees, and that the ability to retain an expensive attorney is regarded as helpful in obtaining justice.

The possibility of great administrative inefficiency in newly self-governing African countries should be regarded in the same light. This will depend largely on the extent and quality of administrative training provided for Africans by the departed colonial power. In Ghana and Nigeria, for example, efficiency seemed to suffer little as a result of independence, partly because so little anti-British bitterness had been left behind, that both Governments recruited substantial numbers of expatriate British civil servants for the period of transition. Ghana had two or three times more white civil servants for the first few years after independence than during the last years of the Gold Coast. Ghana also had about 200 trained African lawyers, and Nigeria 800. British

Central and East African Territories were not so long or so well prepared, and except for Tanganyika, their peoples harbored greater resentment toward the British than did those of West Africa. It would therefore be reasonable to expect a higher incidence of violence, corruption, and inefficiency in the East than the West of Great Britain's former African Empire.

Even if the gloomiest predictions of European colonials sounded as persuasive to African leaders as they do sound to these prophets themselves, the Africans would not be deterred from pushing for immediate and full independence, as indicated by the statement at the opening of this chapter—in an irrefutable way, incidentally, once self-government has been accepted as the ultimate goal. There is another reason for the irrelevance of these predictions of violence, corruption, and inefficiency. Nonviolence, honesty, and efficiency are western values. Africans may share these values to some extent, but they are likely to have different priorities, dictated in part by their unique situation, as they make their simultaneous transitions from dependence to independence, from traditionalism to modernization, from objects of power politics to, occasionally, arbiters between the super-powers in the "age of overkill." Nonviolence, in fact, is a very recent western value. The Europeans' opposition to African violence springs more from the desire to maintain "law and order" than from any Gandhian convictions, especially in the colonies, many of which were "conquered" by military violence. The Africans have no reason to defend the "law and order" of the colonial regime they are trying to throw off. And in other respects, as mentioned earlier, they lack the western and eastern traditions of military glory that have helped to bring about the great wars of this century.

Thus, while Africans may value true nonviolence even more than its colonialist exponents do, it need not occupy the top place in their hierarchy of values. Independence, for their own country, or for other still colonial territories in Africa, occupies that place. This fact lends an aura of unrealism at best, or hypocrisy at worst, to the demands of colonial governments, of white settlers, and in the United Nations of Western states, that leaders of independence movements appeal energetically to their followers to abstain completely from the use of violence. Such appeals were made, for example, to Jomo Kenyatta, Dr. Banda, and Kenneth Kaunda, before their respective arrests. And each did, to some extent, respond favorably to this appeal. It was also made at the UN to the Angolans who were fighting Portuguese settlers and troops in 1961. Its unrealism comes from the fact that independence from colonialism ranks as the most important goal for these Africans. If the leaders were to devote much energy to exhorting their supporters to refrain from violence, they would thereby dilute the impact of their drive for independence.

Premature worry over post-independence corruption and inefficiency would have the same diluting effect. Both of these concerns also involve the frequently heard economic arguments against independence for territories said to be not viable economically. The independence movements are not pursuing economic viability or honesty or efficiency, but independence. Moreover, as in the case of nonviolence, it is likely that their different background and situation give Africans a different attitude toward these values. For example, instead of the impersonal, machine-like honesty and efficiency of the ideal type of Western civil servant, they may prefer public officials who are more "human," approachable, amenable to influence, and leisurely than European civil servants under the conditions of highly industrialized, densely populated, and intensely bureaucratized societies. Different content is given to apparently similar values by the unique condition of the Africans' life.

Western Expectations and Values

The prediction of corruption serves to illustrate the error of perceiving and judging events in the new Africa solely in terms of our concepts and our values. One reason why some African politicians are accused of corruption is the pattern which their careers have often followed. In the democratic West, the normal career of politicians moves from secondary and higher education, through business or professional achievement, to political office. In the new African states, the normal pattern is often the exact reverse. A young man—the average age of African political leaders is relatively very low—first acquires political prominence, perhaps by being thrown in jail by the colonial power; many prison graduates in British territories proudly affix the initials "P. G." to their names. His political career may be interrupted by a year or more at school in Europe, America, or India—or, more recently, behind the Iron Curtain. Or he may move directly into ministerial office. In many cases, African politicians start business enterprises while they are engaged in the effort for independence. This has been true especially in East Africa, where retail trade used to be monopolized by Indian traders until a concerted effort was made, on both Government and African initiative, to create a group of African merchants. Sometimes, European or Indian owned companies ask African politicians to join their boards of directors, and this may give rise to charges of corruption. The same often happens purely in terms of the enormous salaries, by general African standards of income, that members of parliament are paid regardless of race. Especially during the multi-racial stage of parliamentary representation, when African MP's are still elected by an overwhelmingly white electorate, the more radical independence leaders accuse them of being opportunistic stooges, who only want to cash in on a salary of £1,200 a year. And there have been instances where African MP's have used this income in order to establish a business and then retire from politics after independence. Of course, once the independence leaders themselves come into office, their income and standard of living jump to the top level of the European bracket. They live in residences formerly reserved for European officials and have at their disposal all the resources of their Government. Former occupants of both homes and offices may resent this, often by anticipation, and claim that the real objective of the African leaders is not self-government and the improvement of their people's standard of living, but self-improvement and the exploitation of their gullible people.

These arguments do not prevent any African independence movement from pursuing and reaching its goal. In any case, many of these criticisms of African politicians are valid only if we agree that the typical current Western political career pattern should set the norm for the new Africa. If, on the other hand, we realize that the new African states are passing through their equivalents of the English, American, French, Russian, and several Industrial Revolutions at the same time, we might admit that a career pattern which has served the United States well would probably be quite out of place in Kenya or Uganda.

The same applies to the American and general Western belief that a sizeable and solid middle class is a prerequisite of, or provides the best foundation for, constitutional democracy. As a basis for policy, this belief is justified only for us if we want to create mechanical replicas of Western constitutional democracies, or for communists who expect to establish socialism upon the rubble of a bourgeois society destroyed by violent revolution. A realistic appraisal of the situation in most of the new states would reveal that they will not acquire the equivalent of a Western middle class, based on private property, in time for it to help shape their political style and institutions, if ever. But this appraisal need not lead us to pessimistic conclusions unless we assume that constitutional democracy as we know it is the final achievement of man's political genius. It leads the Soviets to equally pessimistic conclusions only if they assume—as they usually do—that their form of socialism is the penultimate achievement of dialectical materialism. Those who advise them should remember that the Africans themselves share neither of these assumptions. They should remember, too, that the social stratum brought into being could not in fact be a middle class, since there would be no upper class, between which and the "workers and peasants" it could mediate.

As part of the Western faith in a substantial middle class, colonial administrators have often sought to convince Africans of the universal beneficence of individual private property in land. With very few exceptions, this was unknown before the arrival of the colonizers. Although there is a great deal of variety in landholding systems, permanent individual ownership and inheritance of real estate by one individual from another was not practiced. Colonial agricultural reformers have frequently tried to introduce individual ownership, in order to bring into being a "class of yeoman farmers," to use British terminology. In most instances, these efforts ran into resistance from the Africans affected. Several leaders of independence movements have asserted that legal reform of the landholding system, far from being a necessary prerequisite for increasing agricultural productivity, would obstruct that goal. They think the establishment of agricultural cooperatives would work more smoothly and bring greater yields if, for example, a tribal or subtribal chief continued to hold the tribe's land in trust and, with the advice of his council and agriculture experts, assigned plots to individuals.

The point of each of these cases—charges of corruption and inefficiency, advocacy of middle class values and institutions—is that Americans would better serve their own national interest and the broader interest of mankind by letting the Africans define their own goals and the order of priority in which they place their goals. The Africans will do this in any case and Americans, by failing to realize it, only generate antagonism. On the other hand, if we recognize the Africans' right to set their own values, as the primary function of independent politics, then we are likely to drop many of our criticisms and our more or less well-intentioned schemes for their improvement.

Tribalism

Even if the reasoning above allays fears about African incompetence for self-government, we still have to deal with predictions of violent conflict between tribes after the restraining force of the colonial administration has been removed. We suggested in the first chapter that the great ethnic and cultural heterogeneity of the new African states might enable them to skip the stage of cultural nationalism that has contributed so heavily to international conflict in the rest of the world. Skeptics generally use this same fact of cultural heterogeneity to forecast inter-tribal conflict within each of the new states. The British East African

Territories—Tanganyika, Kenya, Uganda, and the islands of Zanzibar and Pemba—provide a good case study for testing this prediction. All will have complete self-government by 1964 at the latest. Each of them has a population that is both multi-racial and multi-tribal, and all four of them had trouble arising out of these facts under colonial rule. Yet in the colonial past, the British administration was always able to restore "law and order." Would withdrawal of the colonial power lead to chaos, anarchy, and intertribal bloodshed on a large scale?

Fears of this have been expressed particularly concerning Uganda. In 1962, its population consisted of approximately 6,700,000 Africans, 12,000 Europeans, and 76,000 Asians. In 1862, when the explorers Speke and Grant first established contact with the Kingdom of Buganda, now one of the four Provinces of Uganda, they were surprised to find a well-organized political system there. Its ruler was called the Kabaka, and the people were conscious of a long past, by African or any other standards: the present Kabaka claims to be thirty-fifth in direct line of succession. Fifteen years after the explorers came the missionaries, both Roman Catholic and Anglican, and a decade after that their converts among the Baganda (inhabitants of Buganda) fought what was in effect the last battle in the religious wars that followed the Reformation. Buganda was initially controlled by the Imperial East Africa Company, which received its Charter in 1888, but found the enterprise too expensive. The British Government therefore took over in 1893, Buganda became a Protectorate in 1894, and the Protectorate was extended to the rest of Uganda in 1896.

The country was administered from Buganda. The Baganda are the largest single tribe, but amount to only 17 per cent of the total population. The next largest tribes are the Iteso, Basoga, and Banyankole with, respectively, 9.4, 8.7, and 7.9 per cent of the population.[6] There are at least thirteen main tribes, three of which in the Western Province have institutions somewhat similar to, but not as strong as, those of the Baganda: Bunyoro, Toro, and Ankole. Economically and culturally, Buganda is the most advanced part of Uganda, and the Baganda are generally ahead of the other tribes in their development. By the Agreement of 1900, the British recognized the Kabaka as ruler of Buganda. The British assumed that he ruled "with the advice and consent" of the Lukiko or Parliament, more or less as British Acts of Parliament are "enacted by the Queen's most Excellent Majesty, by and with the advice and consent of the Lords Spiritual and Temporal, and Commons, in . . . Parliament assembled, and by the authority of the same. . . ." Until the Lukiko was made partly elective, by an indirect system, in

⁶ David E. Apter, *op. cit.*, p. 36.

1945, it resembled a feudal council of local lords, who had been given their lands by the Kabaka.

In 1953, there was talk of federating the three East African Territories of Uganda, Kenya, and Tanganyika, which already were under the authority of the East African High Commission for purposes of operating harbors and railways, defense, postal communications, currency, and income tax. 1953 was also the year of the founding of the Central African Federation. In Uganda, there was concern that an East African Federation would mean domination by the white settlers of Kenya, just as Africans in Northern Rhodesia and Nyasaland feared domination by the white settlers of Southern Rhodesia. Buganda, which like Basutoland had become a Protectorate at its own request instead of having been conquered, therefore demanded its own immediate independence, regardless of what was to happen to the rest of Uganda. The ensuing quarrel between the Kabaka and the Governor ended in the deportation to England of the Kabaka, in late 1953. In the course of the controversy, the Kabaka refused to nominate Buganda's representatives to the Legislative Council of Uganda.

The British Government then sent Sir Keith Hancock, a constitutional expert, to Uganda. He recommended that the position of the Kabaka be constitutionalized and that representation in the Uganda Legislative Council be broadened. The Kabaka was permitted to return home after more than a year in exile. Buganda, under the leadership of Kabaka and Lukiko, boycotted elections to the Uganda Legislative Council in 1955, while in the other Provinces about 80 per cent of the eligible voters registered, and 80 per cent of those registered voted. When new elections were held in 1961, Buganda again declared a boycott, although some elected members of the Lukiko ran for and were elected to the Legislative Council. In 1960, the Lukiko had passed "A Memorandum to Her Majesty Queen Elizabeth II Submitted by Members of the Lukiko of the Kingdom of Uganda," requesting termination of British Protection, projecting full membership in the Commonwealth and separate representation at the United Nations for Buganda, but also retention of most connections with the other members of the East African High Commission.[7]

The question of Buganda secession therefore seemed to be the main issue of Uganda politics and Uganda-British relations, since the British Government declared its intention to give Uganda self-government at an early date. However, even if this really were the main issue, it was complicated by several others. In Buganda, there is said to be going on a struggle between traditionalists, whose symbolic head is the Kabaka,

[7] *Ibid.*, Appendix, pp. 479-488.

and the more modern elements of the population, led by the organizers of political parties. Marxists would probably describe this as a struggle between feudal and bourgeois elements. Secondly, several "political parties" have been competing in Uganda politics, mainly for seats in the Legislative Council. These organizations, with very few exceptions, were constantly splintering and regrouping, so that it was almost impossible to keep track of the various individuals and offices. In the elections of 1961, the Democratic Party, which had been accused by its opponents of being a Roman Catholic Party, was most successful, and its leader Mr. Benedicto Kiwanuka, was designated first leader of the House in the Legislative Council (Legco), and then Chief Minister, by the Governor. Mr. Kiwanuka was also an elected member of the Lukiko, whose Speaker suspended him from that body for failure to observe Buganda's boycott of the election; whereupon the Kabaka removed the Speaker, and Mr. Kiwanuka was readmitted to the Lukiko. Meanwhile, the Democratic Party's majority in the Uganda Legislative Council was based on votes cast mainly in the other three Provinces, and a minority even of these (due to distortions caused by the single-member plurality electoral system).

The most divisive issues of Uganda politics thus arose out of a constitutional problem. First, there was the issue of the proper scope of the unit of politics. Three alternatives have been advanced to resolve it: a unitary Uganda, which was unacceptable to Buganda; a federal Uganda, which was unacceptable to the rest of Uganda, whose people are afraid of Baganda domination; or secession of Buganda, unacceptable to both the British and the non-Baganda. Next, there was the issue, most important in Buganda, of traditionalism *versus* modernism. This was not as simple and clear-cut as it sounds. The Kabaka himself is a very modern individual, who received an excellent university education in England. Before 1955, John Gunther could write accurately:

> The offices of the prime minister of Buganda no more resemble those of a corporation executive in New York than a hut in Polynesia resembles the House of Commons. One must never forget the appalling, dismal decrepitude of native Africa, which is caused partly by poverty, partly by the speed and confusion of an overnight transition from medieval to modern times.[8]

But by 1959, because of the speed of change, that same office had become more luxurious than many an executive office in New York, and the new chamber of the Lukiko as beautiful in its own way as, and certainly more modern than, the House of Commons at Westminster. The main

[8] John Gunther, *Inside Africa,* p. 437.

reason for construction of the new Lukiko building, which also houses the Ministers' offices, was competition with the Uganda Legislative Council, for which a new building was also built in time for the election of 1961.

In addition to these issues, there were others still generated by the religious wars of the last century, as well as disagreements between the African majority and the Asian minority, whose stores were boycotted for a year and a half in 1959 and 1960 by Africans trying to break their near monopoly on retail trade. Several of the problems giving rise to the issues seemed to have no workable solutions as of 1961. Some had given rise to violence and violent intimidation in the past. Others, including both tribal differences and the denominational split, had caused civil war in the nineteenth century, and memories of such conflicts are still associated with these issues. The British Government was honestly eager to give Uganda self-government as soon as they could do so safely, that is, without leaving in the lurch the non-Baganda.[9] If we assume that acceptable interim solutions can be found to all these problems, and that the British will be satisfied that they have met their responsibilities, would violence—between Buganda and other Provinces, Africans and Asians, modernists and traditionalists—be likely to break out after their departure? Before we answer this question, we should consider some seemingly equally difficult problems raised by tribalism in East Africa.

Toward an East African "Federation"

The same question about the likelihood of intertribal violence could be asked about Kenya, whose Kikuyu are the most vigorous of all its tribes, even though they are not organized into an equivalent of Buganda's "political kingdom." But both Kenya and Tanganyika share in common the problem of the nomadic Masai, who number less than 100,000, three-fifths of them in Kenya, the rest in Tanganyika. The Masai have been satisfied under British administration, except when it interfered with their hunting practices in order to preserve game in national parks designed to attract foreign tourists. But they objected to being controlled by African governments in Nairobi and Dar-es-Salaam, since these governments of an independent Kenya and Tanganyika would be elected by electorates in which the Masai would be enormously outnumbered: both in absolute terms, and for as long as money income and educational qualifications are retained for the franchise, since the Masai have been

---

[9] This was again demonstrated by publications of the "Munster Report" on Uganda's constitutional future in 1961.

less interested than most other tribes in both of these ingredients of modernization. Representatives of the Masai asked the Governors of both Territories prior to independence to let them set up their own Masai State, which would be formed by carving their pasture lands out of both Tanganyika and Kenya. The Governors rejected these demands as impracticable. The Masai have also been involved in occasional violent clashes with members of other tribes. For instance, outside Nairobi, some Masai attacked a political meeting of the Kenya African National Union, one of the two main African parties engaged in the campaign of 1960, preceding election of the Kenya Legislative Council in 1961. In this election, incidentally, Mr. Tom Mboya, a member of the Luo tribe, was overwhelmingly elected in a constituency most of whose voters were Kikuyu. Even in the face of such hopeful signs, what is to keep the more advanced majority tribes from taking reprisals against, and advantage of, small backward tribes like the Masai?

Similar questions were raised by election violence on the island of Zanzibar in 1961, during which more than sixty people lost their lives. On Zanzibar, the situation was further complicated by the presence of an economically and culturally advanced Arab minority, whose head, the Sultan of Zanzibar, had been recognized as the constitutional ruler of the British Protectorate of Zanzibar and Pemba for seven decades. The Arabs are Muslims, as are many non-Arabs on Zanzibar. So are Somalis living in Kenya near the Kenya-Somali boundary. Spokesmen for these Somalis have demanded that the Kenya territory occupied by them should join the Somali Republic, which came into being in 1960 through union of formerly British Somaliland with the prewar Italian colony and postwar Italian UN Trusteeship Territory of Somalia.

The many difficult problems of this type have made many outside observers pessimistic about the post-independence future of Britain's four East African Territories. This pessimism would seem warranted, if the solutions to these currently most important problems had to be found within the boundaries of each of them; that is, the problem of Baganda separatism within the present Uganda; of Masai backwardness within both Tanganyika and Kenya, with restrictions imposed on their current free movement across the boundary; of African anti-Arab resentment on the two islands alone. But this is not so. The most influential African leaders from all four Territories have indicated that they know that workable solutions to these problems can be looked for on a larger scale, involving at least Tanganyika, Kenya, Uganda, and Zanzibar, and probably other neighboring former colonies as well. Several African politicians from these territories think that the most likely road to success for their separate political systems lies in the creation of more encompassing new political systems. These new systems would be based on both the various communities already existing among them, which cut across their present colonial boundaries, and on new feelings of community that will be brought into being in the future. At least one African leader indicated his willingness to take concrete steps in this direction. Mr. Julius Nyerere, Prime Minister of Tanganyika, the first of these four to achieve full independence, declared in public that his country would be ready to slow down its pace toward independence in order to enable all four territories to reach that goal at about the same time, so that they could emerge into independence as an East African Federation. Mr. Nyerere had also been one of the organizers of the Pan-African Freedom Movement for East and Central Africa (PAFMECA), under whose auspices meetings were held, starting in 1958, of leaders from the four British East African Territories, Nyasaland, the Rhodesias, the Congo, and Ruanda-Urundi (two African kingdoms with political structures resembling Buganda's, which were Belgian UN Trusteeship Territories until 1962). In 1961, the rulers of Ruanda and Urundi negotiated with Prime Minister Nyerere about "federating" their kingdoms with Tanganyika. In the same year, a conference was also held in London on the future of the East African High Commission. It was attended by delegates from Tanganyika, Uganda, and Kenya, and an observer from Zanzibar, and decided to continue the Commission under the new name of East African Common Services Organization. It will be headed by the three (or four, if Zanzibar decides to join) Prime Ministers. Thus, PAFMECA, after it has won "freedom" from colonial rule for East and Central Africa, will work toward the establishment of larger associations that will, for certain purposes, do away with the artificial cages into which colonial boundaries put their subjects.

The African leaders are groping their way in this direction, because they evidently realize that problems like that of the roving Masai herdsmen could not be solved by newly independent African states conducting themselves like conventional sovereign nation-states in Europe. However, if these new states were members of larger associations, and if their members considered "sovereignty" as meaningless as it is becoming even in other parts of the globe, then the problems raised by the existence of the Masai and their peculiar habits might be solved with relatively little friction. Such solutions would probably generate new problems at the level of the new supra-territorial institutions, but these novel problems would be less likely to lead to military conflict than the old ones, because they would not involve the attributes of conventional sovereignty—centralization of military force, territorial frontiers, and national-cultural consciousness. The same applies to Buganda. Within the present Uganda, no way could apparently be found to reconcile the goals and fears of the Baganda, the other tribes, and the British. However, within an

East African or greater association of political systems, a solution might be much easier to find. For example, in those things for which they are feared by the other tribes in Uganda at present, the Baganda would be counterbalanced by several other tribal communities in East Africa, some larger and some smaller than they, some more and others less advanced. There would be no reason to fear the centralization of police and military force in the hands of any single group, because force would not be centralized in this conventional European way. There would be minimum disturbance over the strict definition of boundaries between territories, because territorial frontiers would not be used as barriers behind which nationalistic governments try to differentiate the culture of their populations as much as possible from each other. Nothing like the deliberate creation of, say, German national culture (including its own distinct alphabet) is likely to happen in East Africa, whose peoples already have two common languages, Swahili and English.

In this sense, a pluralism of overlapping public authorities may be spun to cover East Africa and, in time, all of Africa, like a web. These authorities will serve a variety of public communities—geographic, cultural, economic. Just what form and shape these authorities and their associations will take, and what functions they are to perform, will of course be determined by the Africans themselves. Their failure in these efforts can be predicted with certainty only if they make the mistake of trying to copy mechanically from the West or the East.

Pre-independence problems appeared as difficult as they did because outsiders, as well as some Africans who had not yet rid themselves of their dependence upon Europeans, looked at these problems in terms of conventional western categories. The American Founding Fathers would probably have become equally despondent about the future of the thirteen colonies and states, had they tried to transplant European institutions, instead of inventing the new. Nearly all the Africans' most important pre-independence problems have been defined, as it were, as European problems, to which there are often no solutions even in Europe (as in the case of the German-speaking "Austrian" minority in Italian Tyrol). If the Africans began to look at their condition in terms of concepts and categories grown out of that condition and forged by the goals that they are pursuing, they might discover that half the problems do not really exist and that the other half can be solved much more easily than, for example, the problem of European unity.

Chapter VIII

The Congo:
Temperament and Time

Politicians of all the countries of Africa, . . . in spite of frontiers and ethnic differences, we are of one mind and have the same desire to make our continent a happy one, free from anxiety, and from the fear of colonial domination. Down with colonialism and tribalism! Long live the Congolese nation! Long live an independent Africa!

—Patrice Lumumba,
Accra 1958

When I heard of Patrice Lumumba's murder, I wept.
—Dr. Hastings K. Banda

Belgian and British Colonial Policies

In 1957, a Flemish soccer team from Belgium played an African team in Leopoldville before an audience in which Congolese outnumbered Europeans 100:1. The Flemish umpire, apparently unsure of his judgment, reversed some of his decisions when booed by the crowd. Nevertheless, the African team lost. After the game, Africans stoned Europeans, hurting some, and damaging many cars.[1]

This story can well serve as a parable of the mistakes of Belgian colonial policy, especially compared to British policy in territories of a colonial status parallel to that of the Congo in 1957. The British would not have sent an all-white team to play an all-black team. If they had,

[1] Gwendolen M. Carter, *Independence for Africa*, pp. 79-80.

they would have been less likely to let it consist of members of only one of the British "tribes"—English, Scotch, Welsh, Irish, and so forth—i.e., as Belgians, they would have included French-speaking Walloons with the Flemish-speaking Flamands. The umpire would have been perfectly sure of himself, and the crowd would have accepted even adverse decisions politely: the Africans in the crowd would have wanted to demonstrate their mastery of the complicated rules of the game and would have considered this mastery more prestigious than their team's victory. The British emphasis in all their colonies has always been upon training in the *procedures* of government and politics and sports, rather than in the *substance* of economic, cultural, or physical advancement.

By contrast, Belgium and other Continental European colonial powers —if they tried to advance their dependent peoples at all—always placed the emphasis on matters of substance. In the Belgian Congo, no politics whatsoever, either white or black, was permitted until shortly before the grant of independence. Africans were given no experience with the procedures of politics, the methods for resolving issues arising out of the problems their communities faced. The economic advancement of the Congolese, however, often put them far ahead of Africans in neighboring British colonies, like Northern Rhodesia, whose Copperbelt adjoins the equally mineral-rich Katanga Province. On the Northern Rhodesian railway, the job of engine driver was still reserved for Europeans (allegedly because they are more responsible) as late as 1961, but the same trains had been pulled by engines with African engineers on the other side of the border for many years. Belgium's paternalistic policy sought to provide the economic and cultural foundation upon which Congolese self-government might eventually, if only in the very distant future, be based. In effect, Belgium, a typical European "middle class society," tried to create an African middle class in the so-called *évolués* of the Congo. The failure of this policy proves the obverse of President Nkrumah's commandment to his people: "Accept ye first the economic kingdom, and nothing else shall be added unto it." Or, if we were to address it to the colonial power: "Offer ye first economic advancement, and ye shall be lucky to escape by the skin of your teeth."

Comparisons between the Congo and British colonies we have studied so far illustrate parallels in political evolution and style between each colonial power and its colonies. For purposes of this comparison, we can take Belgium as representative of Continental Europe in general. Similarities between Belgium and France, Spain, Portugal, and the Netherlands are at least as strong as the differences between all of these Continental countries, on the one hand, and Great Britain on the other. These differences are reflected, or almost repeated, in their respective colonies in Africa (and before that in the Americas, Asia, and the Near East). They are important enough for us to discuss in some detail three of the main differences between Britain and Belgium "at home," and then to trace their echoes and shadows in Africa.

Timing of Revolutions. In British history, major sets of problems usually arose one at a time and were recognized as most pressing by the politically conscious population. Each was solved at least to *their* satisfaction, and thereby provided a layer of consensus—especially agreement on procedures of debate—which could then be used for dealing with the next single set of serious problems. In broad outline, this is illustrated by the problems lying behind the sequence of religious settlement in the sixteenth century, constitutional settlement in the seventeenth, and Industrial Revolution starting in the eighteenth century. Belgium, by contrast, did not come into existence until the Revolution of 1830 forced dissolution of the Kingdom of the Netherlands, in which the former Austrian Netherlands had been included under Dutch and Protestant rule after Napoleon's defeat. Belgium escaped the Revolution of 1848 through a timely lowering of franchise qualifications, but at the cost of never successfully resolving its great religious, language, and economic issues, i.e., the conflicts between Protestants and Roman Catholics, between Walloons and Flamands, and between opposing economic classes. The religious issue continues to cause occasional violence in connection with questions of government subsidies to church schools. The ethnic issue resulted in violence and demands for an autonomous Wallonia in the great strike that followed the Congo disaster. Belgium's relatively early industrialization caused the founding of a Labor Party in 1885, much labor unrest and, in 1899, a demand by the Liberal-Socialist coalition for "one man, one vote." Although a very liberal constitution was copied from its authors' understanding of "the British Constitution" in 1831, the leaders of unenfranchised or underprivileged Belgians considered admission to Belgian parliamentary politics and identification with its procedures less prestigious than achievement of their substantive economic and cultural goals.

In Britain, popular politics has, as a result, normally been conducted between two major camps, divided on one main set of issues at a time, which could be resolved by means of procedures to which politicians were at least as attached as to their immediate political victory. In Belgium, the public has been politically divided into a number of camps by a number of coincident and equally important issues, conflict over which could not always be contained by the weak prevailing constitutional consensus.

Extension of the Franchise. In Britain, the franchise was extended very gradually, never as a pure gift on initiative from above, always in response to demands and pressure from below. Throughout this process, the same center of authority—the Crown, eventually including the Cabinet—was recognized by all participants. Participation in politics was extended to an ever-widening electorate which could be viewed as a series of ever-widening but always concentric circles. In Belgium it took a political general strike in 1913 to extort universal male suffrage, which was not finally granted until 1919 after World War I. The authority of the Crown was seriously questioned but not altogether dispersed after World War II during the crisis that resulted in the abdication of King Leopold in favor of his son Baudoin.

Legal Systems. The English Common Law and other historical factors combined to let British political institutions and procedures evolve very slowly and gradually, in a haphazard and asymmetrical fashion that permitted old forms to be infused with the new matter for which the great problems of any particular era called. The Belgians, on the other hand, because of Continental traditions of the Roman Law and its great codifications, especially the Napoleonic, have gone in for wholesale constitutional reforms by means of legislation meant to be comprehensive for its field and internally consistent. For example, the Belgian Parliament passed the single and comprehensive *Loi Unique* to deal with all the domestic problems raised by the Congo debacle, and thereby incidentally precipitated the great strike and "intertribal" conflict between Walloons and Flamands. The British Parliament saw no need for any comparable measure after the Suez disaster.

African Echoes of Metropolitan Differences

These three major differences and their effects have their counterparts in British African territories and in the Congo. There are of course great variations from one British colony or ex-colony to the next within a discernible pattern of broad similarities of development. These variations are of great significance themselves, if we compare them with the uniformity of constitutional and political development in France's many former African colonies. (Since Belgium had only the Congo, we cannot compare it in this respect.) We have already seen how the British provided different constitutions, at a varied pace of constitutional advancement, suited to the needs of territories as different from one another as Basutoland, Southern Rhodesia, or Uganda. Faced with similar contrasts in their West and Equatorial African Territories, the French legislated uniform, standardized, and much more centralized constitutions. The Belgians similarly imposed a highly centralized administration upon the Congo, which is one-third the size of the United States, and were very insensitive to differences in the needs and customs of the hundreds of tribes that make up its population of more than 13,000,000.

In British territories, even when an outside observer could recognize several equally important problems at the same time, all the issues arising out of these problems have usually been formulated by the independence movements as though there were only one problem, or at least one problem of such overriding importance that the others had to be subsumed under it. The central issue has usually been that of independence, and African politicians have usually buried their cultural and economic differences until independence was achieved. Often they were well trained in the procedures of parliamentary politics even before they became active in "true" politics, largely because the British unconsciously use these procedures in so many spheres of life that the Africans almost had to "pick them up" from the British just as unconsciously. Most British trained Africans therefore know how to conduct debates at public political meetings. They do not first have to debate the rules to be used for resolving their substantive disagreements.

We have already discussed reflections of different experiences between the French and the British in Africa with extension of the franchise.[2] In the British colonies, political participation extended from the Crown and its representative, the Governor, through the Legislative Council, gradually and in ever-widening concentric circles, in response to demands from the Africans. During the early stages of independence movements, Africans as a result always looked upon admission or election to "Legco," and later membership in the Executive Council, as the main stepping-stone on the way to their ultimate goal. Over the long run, this goal—independence and all the material improvements that they expected to follow from it—was shaped by the parliamentary procedures with which the politicians were gently forced to gain experience. These procedures were adopted even by those "traditional authorities" that continued to exist after British occupation under the policy of Indirect Rule. As a result, even these African governments, like the Kabaka's and Northern Nigerian Emirates, were also fitted smoothly into the series of circles, at the center of all of which stood and stands the British Crown or its successor.

Constitutional advancement for the British colonies was gradual. Very little wholesale legislation took place. Most changes were made through Royal Instructions to colonial governors, or by means of Orders in Council; a very few through Acts of Parliament. Even these, on comparison with their Continental counterparts, stand out by their lack of comprehensiveness, their internal inconsistency, frequent references to older acts, orders, instructions, or treaties of protection.

[2] See pages 92-94 above.

The procedure was very different in the Belgian Congo. After World War II, African advancement proceeded fairly far in the economic and cultural realms, but there was none in the political sphere. The highest status for Congolese was to be considered *évolué*. The Congo was administered under the Law of 1908, a wholesale change from the previous personal rule of the King. Through missionaries and other Belgians resident in the Congo, both the denominational and the ethnic conflicts of the mother country were exported to its great colony. No one had the franchise until December 1957, when mayors of African communes or municipalities were suddenly ordered elected by universal male suffrage. This sudden extension of the franchise did not take place from one stable center, but within various cities and provinces. Nor was there even the kind of coalescing movement, as between stalagmites and stalactites, that took place in many British colonies, where local government was built *up* from the grass or bush roots, while central government was extended *down* from the center of authority provided by Governor, Executive, and Legislative Councils.

The Fundamental Law

With the indecisiveness of the soccer umpire, the Belgian Government twice announced political concessions to the independence movements after African riots. Also, when Belgium produced the *loi fondamental* that served as the independent Congo's first constitution, its authors made a halfhearted effort to let the King of the Belgians continue as joint head of state for both Belgium and the Congo, on the model of the British Crown as the symbolic head of the Commonwealth. The Fundamental Law itself could best be described as a constitutional monstrosity including some of the worst features of some of the least successful of contemporary constitutions, especially the Fourth French Republic and the Italian Republic, with an additional admixture of an impracticable quasi-federalism influenced by the German Federal Republic. It ran to 259 articles, sought to be both comprehensive and consistent, and ended up by being too complex to be operated even by experienced parliamentarians. Some critics of the Belgians accused them of duplicity, suggesting that they designed the Fundamental Law in order to demonstrate the inability of the Congolese to govern themselves, and hoped to be recalled, perhaps as agents for the United Nations, after a short period of disorder. We do not have to accept this suggestion since, as we noted earlier, in such circumstances motives are usually both harder to identify and less interesting to analyze than consequences.

The bias in favor of the substantive and against the procedural was shown throughout the six months before the independence date, suddenly set for June 30, 1960. Writing a constitution for the Congo was considered less important by both Belgians and their Congolese trainees than working out economic plans. Round tables on both topics were held in Brussels. In fact, so many round tables were conducted, that Congolese were dancing to the "Round Table Cha Cha," as well as the Kasavubu and Lumumba Cha Chas. But as late as the middle of May, no copies of the new constitution were available in the Congo's second largest city, Elisabethville. A week before Independence Day, the newly elected Parliament had not yet produced either a Cabinet or a Head of State. Western diplomats, Belgian officials, and foreign correspondents in Leopoldville were unanimously predicting that there would be no Government to which the King of the Belgians could turn over "sovereignty" on June 30, 1960. In view of the Fundamental Law, this sounded like a safe forecast. Parliament consisted of a Chamber of Representatives, elected directly by universal male suffrage from single member districts, and the Senate, to which each of the six Provinces or States indirectly elected fourteen Senators through their directly elected Provincial Assemblies. The Prime Minister and his Cabinet needed the confidence of both houses, unlike most parliamentary systems, in which the confidence of the lower house suffices. Chances were that a Cabinet acceptable to the Chamber of Representatives would be unacceptable to the more "states' rights" or even tribal minded Senate. But even if a Cabinet should manage to win votes of confidence in both houses, the Head of State still remained to be elected, by a two-thirds majority of the members of both Houses in joint session. Even under the Fourth Republic in France an absolute majority of members of the two chambers sufficed to elect the President of the Republic; and in 1953 this process required the casting of thirteen ballots! In the new Congo, this system was supposed to be operated by "parliamentarians" without any experience whatsoever in parliamentary or any other kind of politics, and no academic training in its procedures except for what they may have learned in a "quicky" six weeks' *cours accéléré de formation politique,* given by Belgian jurists with very formalistic inclinations.

In the face of these apparently insuperable obstacles, and after intensive behind-the-scenes negotiations, Mr. Lumumba was voted confidence by both Houses. Mr. Kasavubu, in return for supporting his previous and future antagonist, was supported by Lumumba's backers to be elected Head of State on the very first ballot. Most debates were dignified, rational, and more orderly than most American presidential nominating conventions. The facts that the Lumumba-Kasavubu coalition was brought into being, and that Prime Minister Lumumba was able to include representatives of all "parties" in his Cabinet, spoke well for the political skill of the inexperienced Congolese politicians regardless of all that happened subsequently.

The disorders that led Prime Minister Lumumba to request United Nations help began in the *Force Publique,* the Belgian-officered Congolese security force, which mutinied shortly after Independence Day. This must have come as a great disappointment to the Belgians, though from our point of view it contains an element of historic irony. The Congo Administration was very proud of the *Force Publique* and its plan to commission Congolese as officers in 1964. The soldiers' pay was high, their families were well taken care of in model housing units, and units were either multi-tribal down to the squad level or stationed in regions where they had no tribal relatives. White settlers outside the Congo, too, who had an interest in seeing Congolese independence produce chaos, banked on the *Force Publique* to restore order. The Prime Minister of Southern Rhodesia, for example, predicted a military dictatorship in the Congo immediately after independence, because he considered the *Force Publique* the only stable element in the situation.

The "Struggle for Power"

What followed was usually described as a struggle for power among various Congolese leaders by foreign observers. Actually, however, there was very little power for which these politicians could have struggled, even had they wanted to do so. The *Force Publique* disintegrated. The sometime leader of parts of it, Colonel (later General) Joseph Mobutu, was treated by representatives of some foreign powers as though he were an up and coming Latin American *caudillo* or a South East Asian military dictator. He turned out to be neither. His and his sometime partners', sometime antagonists' soldiers were repeatedly reported to be on the verge of mounting a full scale civil war. The war never took place, although there was sporadic intertribal violence of a type that had preceded independence and had never been entirely suppressed by the colonial administration. Congolese soldiers lacked not only the military equipment with which to conduct major military operations, but the feelings of loyalty to the equivalent of a "sovereign" needed to engender the obedience and organizational discipline without which modern warfare is impossible. Opposition between hostile political factions was not easily capable of clear territorial definition. In fact, both geographical and ideological or merely programmatic definition of the various personalities, "parties," or factions turned out to be equally difficult.

Western observers were confused, for example, when Kasavubu, Lumumba, Tshombe, and others successively denounced and praised the United Nations; when one leader "arrested" another only to emerge together with him from his villa in amiable conversation; when a rapid succession of very definitive sounding deadlines and ultimatums were issued at irregular intervals, only to be utterly ignored by both issuers and addressees; when the murdered Prime Minister's self-styled successor, Mr. Antoine Gizenga, was described as a Soviet trained Marxist, only to expel six Communist reporters from his capital, Stanleyville; and when "strong men" who were expected to kill one another did so in very few instances—then, possibly at the instigation of Europeans— and instead succeeded in talking themselves back together. These reports bewildered most Americans, because they tried to understand the events behind them as though they were a struggle for power like those in France in 1958, 1960, and 1961.

Balkanization

Similar misunderstandings also arose when various "secessionist" movements in the Congo were interpreted as contributing to the inevitable *balkanization* of the Congo and the rest of Africa south of the Sahara. African leaders, especially Drs. Azikiwe and Nkrumah, were first to apply this word to Africa in warning their fellow Africans against the danger of the fragmentation of ex-colonies into a number of smaller territories based on tribal homogeneity. The word stems from the period of disintegration of states in the Balkans following World War I, when various nationality groups claimed the right of self-determination, and the "successor states" to the Austro-Hungarian Empire and their neighbors engaged in a great deal of military action over territorial claims; e.g., Budapest was occupied by Rumanian troops. African fears of balkanization in the sense of fragmentation are often based on the suspicion that some colonial powers, like Belgium and France, are not making genuine withdrawals when they grant independence to their possessions, and will continue to encourage the establishment of many small African successor states. These will retain direct economic links and will therefore return to some form of dependence upon the former colonial power. In any case, the colonial powers may think that many small states will be easier for them to deal with on the international plane than a few larger ones or unions of several of the former colonial territories.

These fears of fragmentation on the part of Africans make better sense than descriptions of recent African events by Europeans as balkanization. In the Balkans during the allegedly parallel period, a great many state boundaries were redrawn, often after military conflict. In Africa, by contrast, very few boundaries had changed between the end of World War II and 1961, except that the borders of colonial territories had become state boundaries as a result of the attainment of statehood. Where new boundaries did come into being, this was the result of application of the old self-determination principle of the League of Nations by the United Nations in the form of popular plebiscites that, moreover, did not lead to the creation of new political entities. Thus the formerly British-administered UN Trusteeship Territory of Togoland joined Ghana instead of the formerly French-administered Republic of Togo. And the southern part of the formerly British-administered Trusteeship Territory of the Cameroons joined the formerly French-administered Republic of Cameroon, while the northern part opted for joining the Federation of Nigeria. Ghana was occasionally accused by Togo of coveting adjacent territory inhabited by members of the Ewe tribe, many of whom live in the formerly Togolese part of Ghana. Whenever this happened, critics of the new African politics pointed with alarm at what they regarded as parallels between it and power politics in the old Balkans. They overlooked that the leaders of these two countries, Presidents Sylvio Olympio and Kwame Nkrumah, periodically met and discussed their differences, reducing the likelihood of major military conflict to a minimum.

In the Congo itself, the initial breaking away of the Province of Katanga and the protracted refusal of Mr. Gizenga and his followers to recognize the authority of the central government of President Kasavubu were also interpreted as symptoms of balkanization. In September 1961, United Nations troops forcibly repatriated more than 100 Belgian and other white officers and non-commissioned officers who had been serving as "mercenaries" with the Katanga army. Without these non-African commanders, its African troops would probably have been unwilling to risk their lives for the cause of an independent Katanga, just as the army of the central government was unlikely to try to enforce Katanga's re-integration into the Congo—that was why the United Nations had to perform this task. That was also why its Secretary General tragically lost his life on his way to negotiations with Mr. Tshombe.

Mr. Gizenga, as Lumumba's heir, was just as much opposed to separatism and tribalism as Lumumba in the exhortation that heads this chapter. He favored reconvening the Parliament that had originally voted confidence in Prime Minister Lumumba's Cabinet. This course was eventually followed, and Gizenga became Deputy Prime Minister in the new Cabinet of Cyrille Adoula, that received an almost unanimous vote of confidence from Parliament. Throughout the period during which the Belgian-designed constitution was in effect, non-African observers usually described Gizenga as favoring a "unitary" Congo and Tshombe as advocating a "confederal" Congo. But these labels are inaccurate, because the emerging constitution of the Congo is unlikely to be either unitary, or confederal, or federal in the accepted meanings of those terms.

President Kasavubu was said to favor federalism for his country, and some of his Congolese and other African critics have attributed this to his "tribalism," as recognized leader of the Bakongo tribe. The Bakongos live along both banks of the Lower Congo River, that is, in the former Belgian and French Congo, and in Angola. In 1960, some of Mr. Kasavubu's lieutenants called for the formation of a new Bakongo State, to be carved out of these colonial territories. In 1961, the Angolan uprising was said to have been initiated by members of the same tribal group, who may have been getting aid, including small arms, from President Kasavubu's followers. The Bakongo are descendants of the highly organized "Kingdom of Congo" which the first Portuguese explorers and colonizers met more than four centuries ago. Their division under at least three different European colonial sovereignties was one result of the "scramble" for Africa. The solution of the problems created by this division, as in the case of similar ones in East Africa, is unlikely to be found by European balkanesque methods.

Shifting alliances between African leaders across the boundaries of the new states suggest that they will not search for solutions by such methods in any case. Occasionally during the long Congo crisis this was, nevertheless, believed to be a major trend; for example, when President Fulbert Youlou of the former French Congo, whose capital Brazzaville is across the Congo River from Leopoldville, seemed to side with his fellow Bakongo, Kasavubu, against Lumumba. In Brazzaville, serious intertribal riots had taken place in February 1959, after the French Congo had voted 99.1 per cent in favor of autonomy within President De Gaulle's new French Community. The fighting was between Bakongo, and M'bochi, and voting in the subsequent election followed tribal lines. Nevertheless, two antagonists of the Abbé Youlou later became Ministers in his Government, though they continued to describe themselves as being "in the opposition." President Youlou took the initiative in convening a conference of independent African states at Brazzaville, whose members—mainly former French colonies—have been referred to as "the Brazzaville Powers." President Youlou also established close relations with Mr. Tshombe of Katanga and apparently broke relations with President Kasavubu when the latter had Tshombe temporarily arrested and charged with treason. At a subsequent conference of independent African states held in Monrovia, Liberia, President Youlou tried in vain to have a resolution adopted urging Tshombe's release and restoration to office. The Monrovia conference was boycotted by the "Casablanca Powers"—Morocco and Egypt, Ghana, Guinea, and Mali—who are united by their common opposition to the later phases of the United Nations' Congo operation, though Ghana kept its troops under UN command in the Congo, while the others withdrew theirs.

These constantly shifting alignments within the Congo and among the new African states make a very confusing impression on Americans, who expect coalitions between ethnic groups in American domestic politics to change only once a generation, and between states in international politics even less often than that. For our purposes, they illustrate the uniqueness of the new African politics, whose processes cannot be described adequately by such conventional terms as "struggle for power" or "balkanization."

African Character and Personality, and *Négritude*

Some scholars explain differences in political behavior by means of "national character." Even if this concept were useful when applied to communities that have been nations for centuries, like the French, it would still be useless in Black Africa. No Congolese national character could have come into existence since June 30, 1960. Nor would it make much sense to speak of Kikuyu, or Lunda, "tribal character" and expect to derive much politically relevant information. This is illustrated by tribes whose members have learned the rudiments of modern politics under different European tutelage. The Lunda, for example, live in Northern Rhodesia, Katanga, and Angola. The Senior Chief of the Lunda in Northern Rhodesia, under British Protection, continued to consider himself loyal to the Paramount Chief or "king" of the Lunda, whose capital was hundreds of miles away in the Congo. But the differences in political behavior of Lunda politicians in Northern Rhodesia and Katanga were striking. In Northern Rhodesia, they were pragmatic, empirical, and rather parochial about their concerns even though often more widely travelled than their Congolese brothers. In all things political—but also in matters not strictly so, like soccer—they made a very British impression, especially in their observance of procedural niceties. The Congolese Lunda, who had been under Belgian rule, were dogmatic, ideological, and much more prone to assertions of universal applicability although they might never have been outside their Province of Katanga. Mr. Tshombe, while campaigning for the Provincial Assembly as leader of the Conakat Party, delivered himself of such statements as, "je suis katangaise fanatique," whereas no African in

Northern Rhodesia would ever say, "I am a fanatic Rhodesian, Zambian, or Lunda." Yet these were sometimes members of the same tribe.

Leaders of African independence movements, out of their opposition to tribalism, naturally had to reject notions of tribal character in that sense. Significantly, they have made no effort to assert the existence or to further creation of anything like a Ghanaian of Senegalese national character. Instead they have advanced the two related concepts of "the African personality" and *Négritude*. The latter has existentialist roots and, to simplify, assumes that Negroes generally have in common at least the discrimination, rejection, and originally slavery, that they have suffered at the hands of white men. "The African personality" has been Dr. Nkrumah's way of expressing similar ideas, but with less philosophical clarity than his French-trained fellows and with perhaps more positive and more political, Pan-African content and intent. These two concepts are of interest to us mainly for the policy intentions that they may reveal. They cannot help us to explain the unique aspects of African politics that have been described.

Judicial Procedures

If national or tribal character are useless for our purposes, perhaps we should concentrate entirely on the political training, if any, that the colonial administration gave its charges. But this would be exaggerating the degree of stability in current patterns of political behavior in the face of all the indications we have seen. The politically conscious people in Africa want—to borrow the slogan of the "New Frontier"—"to move ahead in the 1960's." They are therefore unusually flexible in their political conduct. Although they naturally tend to resemble their colonial trainers somewhat during the transition to full independence, they will adopt and adapt whatever they consider best suited to help them achieve their most important goals.

However, the modernizing Africans rightly do not want to restrict themselves to adopting a variety of modern political techniques, Western and Eastern. Many of their own tribal communities or full-fledged political systems, where such existed, have more or less ancient procedures, especially court processes, which may be adapted to modern political needs. We have noted these judicial and other procedures before, such as the Basuto "Pitso" and the Sunday meeting in the Nyasaland bush. From the latter, we concluded tentatively that African discussions of this type were less "pointed" and less to the point than their presumed Western counterparts. The Devlin Commission *Report* itself recognized the likelihood that the meeting did merely discuss; that is, almost like a "gripe session," the discussion was not directed toward culmination in action.

Political, parliamentary, and quasi-parliamentary procedures in the West—and in those parts of the East under Western influence—are designed to resolve the issues arising out of problems faced by a community. This resolution results in action, that is, in the solution of the problem. At least since the revolution in military techniques that preceded the Industrial Revolution, the need has been for fast action, in a social environment whose members are always very conscious of the passage of time. In tropical Africa, even as it is rapidly modernizing, there is much less awareness of the passage of time.

In tropical, tribal Africa there was until recently little need for swiftness or novelty of action. Rarely were any new problems recognized as true problems, that is, as removable obstacles between the community and its goals. This was, and in many tribal situations still is, true even of judicial proceedings. Here we might think there is a need for action, and preferably for speedy action. Two parties to a law suit would probably not go to court, unless there were a real conflict between them that threatened to erupt into violence. Unless the issue of this conflict were resolved by the court, everyone in the tribe or village might take sides and the "domestic tranquillity" of the community would be disrupted. However, if we look at African tribal courts in these terms, we may be misunderstanding their functions and misrepresenting what goes on in them.

It is quite possible—even in the United States—for two or more individuals to go to court, not because they are about to hurt or kill each other, but because they are bored, because there is little entertainment in the bush (or the tenement house). Court provides an unequalled opportunity to achieve local prominence and to display dramatic talents before an interested local audience. Many tribal courts seem to perform just such functions: general entertainment, opportunities for self-dramatization, and general airing of grievances and other emotions and views. This may be one explanation for the fact that, contrary to western court practice, some African courts never get around to a fairly clear statement of what is at issue between the parties. Nor does the "verdict" necessarily find one party in the right, the other in the wrong, and direct the guilty party to perform specific action under sanctions of force. Instead of bringing specific force to bear upon a particular point at issue, we get the impression that the "court"—often consisting of a large part of the community involved—has slowly built up a consensus that is spread, as it were, over the whole community. At the end, everyone is more or less satisfied, at any rate more satisfied than he was at the beginning. The process probably consumed a great deal of time. No violence or threats of violence are necessarily raised throughout the proceedings.

Whether this is an accurate description of original tribal courts is impossible to tell, because all the accounts we have were seen through Western or Westernized eyes, whose owners were looking for parallels to what goes on in Western law courts. Social anthropologists usually collected cases tried by African courts after the colonial administration induced the "native authorities" regularly to write down a condensed record of each case. The standard categories of these records were of course taken from Western legal practice: plaintiff, defendant, charge, issue, verdict, sentence or fine, and so forth. The very fact that they had first learned the habit of writing things down must have made the proceedings more precise than they were originally. At the same time, these records probably also omit important parts of the trial. Moreover, most of the courts observed by social anthropologists in this century were also operating as low-level judicial arms of the colonial administration.

To sum up, Africans have a hard time understanding us and the Europeans, in either our domestic or international politics, when we look upon politics as the process designed for the quick resolution of clearly defined issues consisting of alternative courses of action, where one must choose *either* the one *or* the other. They may instead look upon politics, as well as the law, as a more or less entertaining process designed to restore old and build up new consensus. There has been nothing in the environment of tropical Africa to make them think in precise and differentiated terms. They may be quite incapable of seeing life as consisting of series of alternative courses of action, between which they have to choose instead of being able to find a middle ground and round off the edges of irreconcilability.

Timelessness

These factors also contribute to giving most Africans an attitude toward time that can be quite exasperating to outsiders, especially to Americans, who are noted for their lack of patience. We mentioned the ultimatums issued in the course of the Congo crisis earlier. One of these was made by Prime Minister Lumumba to the Belgians remaining in Leopoldville. He had ordered them out once or twice before, when he told General Alexander, the British Chief of the Ghana Defence Staff, who was then in charge of UN military operations, that the Belgians would have to get out by five o'clock that evening. General Alexander looked at his watch and said, "But it is already half past five, Prime Minister." Lumumba, quite unfazed, replied, "That, General, is your problem, and I leave you to deal with it in your wonted fashion."

There are good reasons for this attitude. In tropical Africa, life has a timeless quality about it. There are no sharply distinctive seasons to speak of, in many places not even the rainy and dry seasons. Days and nights are of equal length near the equator, throughout the year. Children do not grow up on a schedule—getting their formulas as babies, having bells rung every hour on the hour in kindergarten, school, military training, or under what Thorstein Veblen called the "discipline of the machine process." Many African languages contain neither numbers, nor anything to give the hour of day more precisely than "the time when people talk" or "when the sun rises." Of course, all of this can be and is being learned. As urbanization, education, and industrialization—in short, modernization—spread, time-consciousness will make the Africans as impatient as it has made us. Meanwhile, however, we must remember that their own peculiar conception of time underlies much of their thinking, their actions, and their politics.

The "African" conception of time is important in another respect. Most of Black Africa is relatively underpopulated, since sufficient land was available for the needs of the local population, at least until colonization. Many of the tribes were more or less nomadic. Those that were primarily agricultural, often used shifting methods of growing crops. Having used one plot of land for a number of years and exhausted the soil, they would leave their villages, move to another spot, and repeat the process. As a result, nothing could develop among them like the European peasant's feeling of obligation to pass on his land in good condition to his descendants, because he had inherited it from his ancestors. (This helps account for the soil conservation troubles, as well as for the relatively low concern with territorial frontiers.) People whose own consciousness of their past is short and shallow usually cannot project their future very far. In fact, past and future are of about equal length in the consciousness of most human beings and of most communities. Widespread illiteracy has also contributed to this lack of depth in memories of the African past, that is, to the lack of historical consciousness. This has benefited African politics by permitting a widespread willingness to experiment with novel institutions and techniques that seems wholly absent in most Asian countries, whose leaders have constantly to ask how any innovation fits into millenia-old customs, traditions, and taboos. Whereas older political systems all over the globe are troubled by elements of bitterness and recrimination for centuries after a particular issue first arose, the new ones in Africa rarely suffer from the stultifying and divisive effects of such negative memories.

African politicians seem to have a great capacity to forgive and forget even their worst enemies.

It is hard to estimate just how these older propensities, derived from their environment and tribal procedures, are going to mix with the modern techniques that the Africans have had imposed upon them or are now adopting and adapting on their own. Even harder to gauge is how this "mix" will affect the procedures and the style of world politics, as more and more independent African states become actors on that stage (which all the world is at the United Nations). The survival of old tribal procedures in their pure form is impossible, even were it desired by the Africans, because of the imperative need for resolution and resoluteness, for solutions to pressing problems, and for speedy reaction to the accelerating course of events.

Chapter IX

French Africa:
The Civilizing Mission

Accomplishment of the goals of civilization by France in her colonies removes any idea of autonomy and all possibility of evolution outside the unity of the French Empire; the eventual establishment of self-government, even in the distant future, is to be dismissed.

—The Brazzaville Conference
(1944)

This state of Mali will assume what some call a "position of independence" and which I prefer to call that of "international sovereignty." . . . A country in order to play its role in the world must follow the paths permitting it to do so; the first of these paths is that it constitutes itself a State. . . . There have been vicissitudes in the history of France but continuity in this history exists and goes back before the Revolution. . . . From its very inception the vocation of France, the purpose of France, have been a humane vocation and a humane purpose.[1]

—President De Gaulle
(1959)

French Centralism

No whites "settled" in West Africa. Various parts of its coast used to be known as "the white man's grave," and some wit has suggested that newly independent West African states should erect monuments to the malaria-carrying mosquito, because it kept the white man out. The

---

[1] From an Address to the Federal Assembly of Mali (1959), quoted in Roy C. Macridis and Bernard E. Brown, *The De Gaulle Republic: Quest for Unity*, pp. 375-376.

absence of white settler communities and other problems of multi-racialism should have made the transition to independence easier for West Africa than for East and Central Africa. In fact, with the exception of Cameroon—where armed clashes occurred before and after independence between government and opposition forces—none of the French or British territories in West Africa had even mild equivalents of Mau Mau or Rhodesian Emergencies. And yet Ghana and Kenya will have achieved independence within a few years of each other, Cameroon and Tanganyika within only two. This again suggests that the internal, African obstacles on the road to independence are of much lower importance than the external, international pressures toward self-govern-

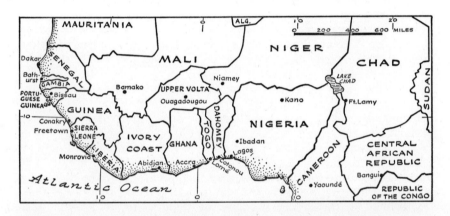

ment. Another pointer in the same direction is the close final timing of full independence for Great Britain's West African and France's West and Equatorial African colonies. Ghana became a full-fledged member of the Commonwealth in 1957. In 1958, with the exception of Guinea, France's African possessions opted in favor of "autonomy" within the new French Community.

France's empire south of the Sahara consisted of French Equatorial Africa (today the Republics of Gabon, Congo, Chad, and the Central African Republic); French West Africa (today the Republics of Niger, Dahomey, Upper Volta, Ivory Coast, Mali, Senegal, Mauritania, and Guinea); and the United Nations Trusteeship Territories of Cameroon and Togoland. The diversity of peoples and conditions in this Empire was at least as great as in Great Britain's African possessions. Nevertheless, we can much more easily discuss all of these former French colonies in this chapter, than deal with only two former British colonies, Ghana and Nigeria, in the next. The main reason is the centralism and uniformity of French colonial administration. We have already commented upon the infinite variety—through variations upon the same theme of gradual constitutional advancement—of British administration in Africa. In France's colonies, uniformity prevailed instead of variety, and constitutional advancement came by leaps and bounds.

In this respect, colonial experience again repeated that of the metropolis. French democracy was highly centralized and unitary, from its inception in the Great Revolution directed against the even more highly centralized *ancien régime*. Local government, which was never as democratic or effective as in the English-speaking countries, was legislated into being from Paris. In the United Kingdom, by contrast, local government grew from the bottom up, while national government was slowly constitutionalized and, later, democratized from the top down. The British repeated this pattern in their African territories, where Lord Lugard eventually rationalized it, in characteristic British fashion, after it had already been experimented with pragmatically. But the British by no means adhered consistently to this rationale, called Indirect Rule—even in Nigeria where Lugard first introduced it formally. The French, on the other hand, legislated uniformly for their African colonies, from Paris, trying to create African replicas of metropolitan institutions.

At the local level, these copies of French models were ill-suited to African needs and political capacities, with perhaps one exception. The exception consisted of four *communes* including Dakar, the capital, in Senegal, whose residents became full-fledged French citizens in 1848, represented in the French Chamber of Deputies by an African since 1914. Elsewhere in French West and Equatorial Africa, Africans could qualify for full equality with metropolitan French citizens through complete assimilation to French civilization. This was how France went about her self-imposed *mission civilisatrice*. How difficult it was to become fully assimilated to French culture in this sense is shown by the fact that, in 1936, only 2,136 Africans out of a West African population of about 14,000,000 had acquired French citizenship through naturalization.[2] The number was this small despite the major benefit of exemption from the *indigénat* that came with naturalization.

The *indigénat* subjected "Natives" to a summary type of criminal jurisdiction at the hands of French colonial administrators. This again contrasts sharply with the British practice of letting traditional authorities continue to apply "native law and custom," even in criminal cases up to a point, and of using African lay "assessors" in district commissioners' courts to advise on local customs. When British colonial

[2] Virginia Thompson and Richard Adloff, *The Emerging States of French Equatorial Africa*, p. 40.

judges reversed the verdicts of African courts, they often used the phrase, "contrary to reason and natural justice." On analagous occasions, their French colleagues used the phrase, "contrary to the principles of French civilization." In practice, this had a more precise and more substantive meaning than its British counterpart, in keeping with the French tradition of substantive justice, as contained in the comprehensive, systematic, and symmetrical Code Napoléon.

The distinction between French citizens and French subjects was abolished when the Constitution of the Fourth Republic was adopted in 1946. This Constitution stressed again the unitary character of the French State and its "Union" with France's overseas territories, and asserted that

> France, faithful to her traditional mission, proposes to lead the people of whom she has assumed charge to a state of freedom in which they administer themselves and conduct their own affairs democratically.

The logic of centralism led to the inclusion of 83 overseas deputies in the National Assembly of 627, and 71 overseas senators in the Council of the Republic of 317. French West Africa elected 20 deputies and 20 senators, Equatorial Africa six deputies and eight senators. In addition, these two "Federations" were represented in the Assembly of the French Union by 27 and 7 councillors, respectively. Within each colonial territory, General Councils were elected by two colleges corresponding, in effect, to the upper and lower rolls of the Southern Rhodesian franchise. The lower roll was open to twelve categories of Africans, among them civil servants, veterans, and heads of African communities. In 1951, three new categories were added to this: heads of households, mothers of two children, and state pensionnaires. As a result, the number of registered voters increased as much as fivefold in some territories. Between the territorial and the French national levels, federal Grand Councils were elected by the General Councils, one for French West Africa with its capital in Dakar, the other for French Equatorial Africa, with its capital in Brazzaville. Many an African leader served simultaneously in the territorial, federal, and French National parliaments, and as mayor of a sizeable city, thus emulating the model of French parliamentarians. This again differs markedly from the British colonies, none of which has ever elected an African, European, or, for that matter, American Member of Parliament to represent it in the House of Commons at Westminster. All the training in practical politics that British Africans got was given them either explicitly in the small legislative councils that were replicas of the great model in England, or implicitly by associating elsewhere with Britons whose procedural conduct they then more or less consciously tended to copy. In the Fourth Republic, on the other hand, a considerable number of African leaders was constantly participating in metropolitan politics right in Paris. As deputies, senators, and councillors they played important roles, not only because they obviously represented their black constituencies, but because they were occasionally able to tip the scales in those delicate maneuvers leading to the overthrow of an old or the formation of a new cabinet—in which African deputies and senators were often included.

In 1956, after the loss of her Indochinese colonies that had been preceded by costly military operations, grants of independence to the North African Protectorates of Morocco and Tunisia, and the beginning of the Algerian war, France suddenly pushed her sub-Saharan colonies over another major hurdle by means of the *loi-cadre*. This "framework law" introduced universal suffrage on a single electoral roll for direct elections to all the West and Equatorial African Territories, transferred many functions previously exercised by colonial or metropolitan administrations to the General Councils, which now elected largely African "Councils of Government" that began to act as proto-cabinets, first under the Governor, then led by the elected African vice-president. In this way, constitutional advancement was given to the colonies both uniformly and in excess of minimum concessions that probably would have satisfied the African politicians. These, because of their participation in French domestic politics during the preceding decade, had not only built up alliances between French political parties and trade unions and their African counterparts, but also transplanted the general pattern of French politics to their several territories. In view of the ideological commitments and interest cleavages that fragmented French domestic politics under the Fourth Republic, one might reasonably have expected this transfer to have had harmful effects on the emerging political systems, and we shall consider below whether subsequent events justified these expectations.

Meanwhile, however, the failure of the Fourth Republic to solve France's most important problems—especially the Algerian war—led to General DeGaulle's return to office, in May 1958, first as Premier and architect of the Constitution of the Fifth Republic, then as elected President. In France, this Constitution was ratified by a margin of 4:1 in a popular referendum. In the African colonies, too, General DeGaulle, in a gesture worthy of the grandeur he intended to restore to France, had referenda held on the Constitution, on September 28, 1958. Only the voters of Guinea voted "no," achieved complete independence as a result, and also lost all French economic and administrative support. All the other electorates voted "yes," by much greater margins than in France herself, and gained the status of "Autonomous Republics" and member states of the French Community, as the successor to the French Union was called, in a not very successful attempt to bring into being a *Commonwealth à la française*.[3] Within two years, the French Constitution was amended to make possible complete independence, instead of mere autonomy, with continued membership in the Community, and all the Autonomous Republics took this choice, mainly perhaps in order to gain direct representation at the United Nations. Similar motives also contributed to the failure of efforts to organize formal federations, like the one between Senegal and the later Republic of Mali (formerly French Sudan) in the Federation of Mali, and another among the former territories of the Equatorial Federation, with the exception of Gabon, that was to have been known as Union of Central African Republics (U.R.A.C.). In this way France, in contrast to Great Britain, on French initiative, without a long-range plan of constitutional advancement, pushed her sub-Saharan colonies into independence by means of several large but irregularly timed leaps.

Liberty, Equality, Fraternity

Throughout this process, until shortly before its conclusion in 1960, the avowed goal had always been the total assimilation to French civilization of France's African citizens. Assimilation was conceived of in substantive terms, as also by the Belgians. But where the Belgians emphasized economic advancement, the French stressed cultural assimilation. Their success in this respect, though confined to the tiny African elite, was remarkable:

> Léopold Senghor of Senegal was a poet, Bernard Dadié of the Ivory Coast a novelist and Cofi Gadeau a playwright, Keïta Fodéba of Guinea a producer of ballets, *before* they held office in their respective states.[4]

But the French, like the Belgians, may have done "their" Africans a disservice through this emphasis on substantive matters and their consequent failure to give more people greater experience with the pro-

[3] L.-S. Senghor, *African Socialism*, p. 9, quoted by Thomas Hodgkin and Ruth Schachter, *French-Speaking West Africa in Transition*, p. 404. Guinea voted "no" by 636,281 to 18,012 "yes." In the Ivory Coast, 1,595,238 voted "yes" against only 216 "no." In Dahomey, 418,963 voted for the Constitution against 9,246. In Upper Volta, 1,415,651 voted "yes," 11,687 "no." In Niger, 372,383 "yes," 102,395 "no." In Senegal, 870, 362 "yes," 21,901 "no." In the French Sudan, 945,586 favored the Community, 23,875 opposed it. In French Equatorial Africa, the "yes" vote exceeded 88 per cent. See Roy C. Macridis and Bernard E. Brown, *op. cit.*, p. 208.

[4] Hodgkin and Schachter, *op. cit.*, p. 387; italics supplied.

cedures of politics. This emphasis is even more misplaced in Africa today than in Europe, because of the rapidity with which the problems faced by the new states are changing, and the radical nature of the changes involved. For instance, 100 per cent agreement in 1960 on the desirability of immediate independence will be of little use in 1962, when independence is a relatively old achievement—unless the people retain at least, say, 70 per cent agreement on the procedures by means of which they can resolve their next substantive disagreement, on tribal differences, the budget, or relations with immediate neighbors, Israel, the Soviet Union, or the United States.

However, the French were almost predestined to direct their colonial efforts toward such goals, and the results can in some respects well stand comparison with those achieved by the British. Ever since their Great Revolution, French Republican regimes have at least pretended to be acting in pursuit of the great goals of the Revolution: liberty, equality, fraternity. Even French colonial administrators who may have been less than sincere about such professions became, to a greater or lesser extent, victims of this revolutionary propaganda slogan. This belief made a policy of assimilation almost unavoidable. Where the English-speaking peoples believed in the rights of Englishmen, or of American federal citizens, the French proclaimed the universal rights of man, not Frenchmen. Where Bills of Rights in the English language only instituted specific negative prohibitions upon organs of Government, i.e., "Congress shall pass no law . . . ," the "Declaration of the Rights of Man and the Citizen" of 1789 used broad positive language:

> Forgetfulness or scorn for the rights of man are the only causes of public misfortunes and the corruption of governments.
> Men are born free and remain free and equal in rights; social distinctions can only be founded upon common utility.

The English-speaking peoples slowly won or extorted from their governments their rights in concrete form, and the governments, as we noted before, never gave rights away as gifts, but made concessions in response to pressure from below, usually just on time, rarely prematurely. The French Declaration of the Rights of Man and the Citizen was not the product of this kind of process. It and its successors stated rights as universally valid for all men everywhere and, therefore, not in the easily understandable and effectively enforceable formulation of negative prohibitions upon government. This meant that France was really committed from the beginning to a nondiscriminatory race policy, whereas Great Britain carried the "white man's burden" for much longer. It also helped to make race relations between the French and their African charges and, later, fellow-citizens much more relaxed. But by positing full equality as the norm, the French had to concentrate on full assimilation, in the substantive cultural sense, of a smaller segment of the whole African population, while the British were able to give political experience and training to a much larger proportion, since they never considered cultural assimilation either feasible or desirable. After independence, the former French territories, whose constitutions incorporated *verbatim* the revolutionary Declaration of Rights, also placed less emphasis on citizens' equality in the sense of "due process" than the former British colonies. The French constitutions talk of the form of government as "a republic, indivisible, laic, social," again reflecting the substantive emphasis of the French and general Continental tradition.

In this respect, too, the policy of cultural assimilation succeeded, although African leaders had begun to criticize it during the early postwar period. They accused the French of syphoning off the elite through an assimilation so thorough that its objects retained little in common with their uneducated, unassimilated fellow Africans. As a result, a reaction set in to the philosophical assumptions upon which assimilationism had been based, especially to the tenet declaring the universal and radical equality of all human beings. In very French fashion, this reaction, too, was provided with its philosophical elaboration in the concept of *négritude*, mentioned above. This view asserts that black men are different from white men, because the whites have exploited them and discriminated against them, causing the conditions of their existence to be different. To impose upon them the same institutions that work in European political systems does the Africans injustice in one direction, just as much as the discriminations of color bar do in the other.

Unintended Consequences of Political Assimilation

The revolutionary founders of the first and later French Republics until the Fifth always failed in their efforts to give France political stability by copying the widely admired parliamentary institutions and procedures of Great Britain. One reason for these failures was faulty copying of a misunderstood model—the sort of error that the American Founding Fathers did not commit. The attempt to transfer parliamentary procedure from Westminster to Paris illustrates this. British procedure is well suited for the conduct of deliberation, that is, the weighing of alternative courses of action. The main function of the House of Commons consists of deliberation upon policies proposed to it by the Cabinet which, under the British constitution, provides continuous resolution, that is, the actual determination of policy. French parliamentary procedure in the National Assembly of the Fourth Republic was also well designed for deliberation, because it had been copied from the House of Commons. But the National Assembly until 1958 mainly needed a cabinet to provide resolution from within it, since there was no such organ in the French constitutional structure. By failing to distinguish clearly between these two phases of the political process, deliberation and resolution, and by providing itself with deliberative procedures despite its resolving function, the French Parliament performed neither task satisfactorily. In the end, it abdicated its task to General De Gaulle, whose Constitution of the Fifth Republic did not repeat such mistakes. In the confusion of the Fourth Republic, however, France's African elite received its political experience.

At first glance, we would expect similar confusion to be perpetuated in the former colonies as a result. In fact, however, this did not happen because, though the General Councils and Grand Councils did use Parisian deliberative procedures, the basic constitutions of the French colonies were quite different from that of France. In each colony, there always was a continuous, stable, and energetic resolving organ in the office of the Governor (or Governor-General), while such an organ was lacking in France. The essentially deliberative procedures of the French Parliament were therefore much better suited for Abidjan and Brazzaville than for Paris. And this continued to be true after autonomy and, later, independence, for three main reasons.

To begin with, there was the carry-over from the initial consensus on the desirability of independence—even though the French were able to prevent the kind of "nationalist" unity from being built up that faced the British in most of their possessions. Contrast this consensus, which also extended to the goal of modernization, with the many deep cleavages that have always criss-crossed French political consciousness at home. To put it differently, even *if* African parliaments had to create cabinets in addition to carrying on deliberation, this would not be as difficult for them as it was for the National Assembly under the Fourth Republic, simply because the African assemblies are not as disunited as that always was.

The second reason is related to the first. Just as the colonial governor provided resolution in each colony before independence, so the premier or president under whose leadership independence was achieved continued to provide resolution afterwards, as head of the government and/ or the state. The creation of new cabinets after the overthrow of old ones will not be a major problem for the new African states, as it was throughout the Third and Fourth Republics. It also ceased to be a major problem for the Fifth Republic, not because French opinion was any less divided after 1958 than before, but because the De Gaulle Constitution clearly segregated resolution from deliberation through the design of the new Presidency and other constitutional devices. The new constitutions of the former French colonies in Africa were written just after De Gaulle's, and some reflect this change in French constitutional design, for example, by requiring a two-thirds vote to overthrow a cabinet, or by providing for the automatic passage of government-sponsored bills unless they are rejected by a specified majority in parliament.

The third reason why this exercise in "political institutional transfer" —to use Professor Apter's description of Britain's launching of Ghana[5] —had unintended consequences is related to the general African preference for and propensity to prolonged deliberation, discussed in the preceding chapter. This may have enabled African politicians to adjust to French deliberative procedures more successfully than the French themselves, whose propensity to strict logic has so often been commented upon by, among others, students of colonialism.[6] Use of these procedures in their new African setting may facilitate true deliberation, in terms of the interests represented in parliament or in an open-ended single party, upon policies resolved and proposed by the leadership of the government and/or party, in a way reflective of prevailing consensus on the goals of modernization. It has already made possible the inclusion in cabinets of leaders of groups which, under the British system, would have to be labelled "the Opposition." As a result, instead of dramatizing and thereby magnifying disagreements, existing consensus will be strengthened. Ghana's constitutional reform of 1960, as the first genuinely African attempt to blend modern with adapted indigenous political forms, also suggests that Africans place a high value upon nonoppositional deliberation, in both government and party, as we shall see in the next chapter. In this one respect, therefore, African countries with a French political heritage may unintentionally have an advantage over their neighbors who were trained in politics by the reputed masters of political science, the British.

Commonwealth *à la française?*

In other respects, however, the French discovered that their desire, inspired by Roman Law, for comprehensive and consistent legislation was less useful than its British counterpart. This fact was probably first brought home to them during the Indochinese conflict and the

[5] David E. Apter, *The Gold Coast in Transition,* pp. 8f.

[6] See, e.g., Thomas Hodgkin, *Nationalism in Colonial Africa,* "French Cartesianism," pp. 33-40.

subsequent loss of colonies. This loss, incidentally, made operative a peculiar French version of the colonial refugee complex, discussed above.[7] By means of, first, the *loi-cadre* and, later, the French Community, the French tried to legislate into being their replica of the Commonwealth. One may wonder how optimistic General DeGaulle himself was about this part of his experiment in constitution-building. It seems at least conceivable that DeGaulle devised the Community as the best means for "putting over" African independence on the French electorate. In any case, the French Community will probably be long outlived by the multi-racial, multi-national, multi-continental, and multi-constitutional Commonwealth, whose members often pursue antithetical substantive policies, but do so always by means of the same stable yet flexible rules.

Adaptations of these rules and of their combinations with African procedures are more likely to be of service in efforts to forge larger associations of communities in Africa. The abortive Federation of Mali, between Senegal and the former French Sudan, had been constructed in a very formal and legalistic way, with typically Continental regard for the niceties of sovereignty and other jurisprudential distinctions. These un-African concepts proved too sandy a foundation, and the Federation collapsed without—to the great credit of both Senegalese and Sudanese—a shot fired. Similarly, the Africans have found their French-taught ideologies, especially socialism and communism, increasingly irrelevant to their own problems. But because they had gone to school in French politics, they started out with greater ideological commitment than their British-trained neighbors, whose teachers were much more pragmatic. As a result, politicians in the former French territories had a harder time emancipating themselves from European ideologies and continued to be more receptive to ideological, as distinguished for the moment from practical, economic overtures from the Soviet Bloc.

This receptivity may turn out to be greater on the part of the second generation of politicians than of the first, who led their countries to autonomy. In the first generation, there were many intellectuals, as we have seen, and other "middle class" types, like Félix Houphouet-Boigny, a physician and planter, minister in French Cabinets, and leader of the Ivory Coast. Houphouet-Boigny became an opponent of his neighbor to the west, Sekou Touré, who led Guinea out of the Community, and his neighbor to the north, Mobido Keïta, who linked his Republic of Mali with Guinea and Ghana after the break-up of the Mali Federation. Under Ivory Coast leadership, he tried to bring into being the rather loose "Union of the Entente," consisting of his home state and the

---

[7] See pages 88-90.

Republics of Upper Volta, Niger, and Dahomey. Houphouet-Boigny, President Senghor of Senegal, and President Youlou of the Congo (Brazzaville)—a doctor, a poet, and a Catholic priest—were regarded as pro-Western moderates by the Western powers. Their careers had reversed those of most of their English-speaking counterparts; that is, they went from substantive accomplishments into politics. Many of this first generation of French-speaking leadership had arrangements with French administrators who were more inclined than their British counterparts to corruption and the use of repressive violence. The African politicians, after they came into office, occasionally used similar methods to deal with their own actual or potential opposition.

The next generation of leaders will in any case lean more toward ideologism than their contemporaries in former British territories, because of the orientation of their French-inspired education. But these leanings may be reinforced, if the "moderate" leaders of the first generation keep the more "radical" younger men from effective participation in politics. Exclusion from meaningful political responsibility usually makes people more doctrinaire. Moreover, this kind of exclusion was more likely to happen in the "moderately" led new states than in Ghana and Guinea, because they were run by "patron" rather than "mass" parties. Unlike mass parties, patron parties made no effort to seek "the adherence of every single individual," but only of "influential notables or patrons." [8] If, therefore, the incumbent moderates should be replaced, their younger successors may turn out to be not only less skilled than their British-trained counterparts in compromising on their internal and intra-African differences, but also more susceptible to Soviet ideological blandishments.

Four other related facts also suggest that the French political heritage and the French Community will have effects less beneficial than the British political heritage, and will be less enduring than the Commonwealth. The first is the initiative taken by former British territories in bringing about wider cooperation among the new African states. We have already mentioned Ghana's leadership in creating the Ghana-Guinea-Mali "Union." But among the members of other groupings, like the "Brazzaville States" or certain African caucuses at the United Nations, Nigeria frequently played a leading role, presumably because its politicians, newly turned diplomats, were better prepared for the conduct of contemporary diplomacy than their colleagues. The latter, who spoke the outmoded language of diplomacy, had been taught by the masters of an older school of diplomacy, whose eighteenth century text was no longer being read anywhere but in France.

[8] Ruth Schachter, "Single-Party Systems in West Africa," *American Political Science Review*, LV, No. 2 (June 1961), 295.

The second fact pointing in the same direction is President DeGaulle's cavalier treatment of and contempt for the United Nations. He disdained the General Assembly perhaps because it reminded him of the ill disciplined French National Assembly of the Fourth Republic. France voted in support of Belgium in the debates of the Congo crisis, perhaps out of feelings of solidarity with its French-speaking neighbors, perhaps out of fear that an unfragmented Congo would overshadow the much smaller African members of its Community, as was alleged by some critics of French policy. France also joined the Soviet Union in its refusal to bear its share of the costs of the United Nations Congo operation. This attitude was unlikely to be well received by the new African states with their strong commitment to the United Nations, the more so because France expressed it during the very session of the General Assembly that had just been joined for the first time by so many members of the French Community.

France's refusal to let the United Nations "interfere" in the Algerian War and President DeGaulle's treatment of the UN and its Secretary General during the Tunisian crisis over the French naval base of Bizerte, together with the substance of these two North African conflicts, are the third factor. The bloody clash in Bizerte, especially, had disruptive effects on the Community, because President Bourguiba of Tunisia had previously played the role of mediator between France and her allies on the one hand, and the Algerian Liberation Movement and other African states on the other. During the Congo crisis, for example, the Tunisian Ambassador to the United Nations occasionally leaned so far toward the "Western" position, that Ghana's and Guinea's diplomats condemned him as a "colonialist stooge" or "imperialist lackey," in private if not in public. They did condemn France's retention of her base at Bizerte as a manifestation of neo-colonialism, and the events of July 1961, in their own view, proved them right and made it easy for them to secure the election of the Tunisian ambassador, Mr. Mongi Slim, as President of the General Assembly of the United Nations.

The fourth and final factor working against the durability of the French Community was the Sahara. France had exploded her first atomic bombs in the Desert, over vehement protests from the formerly British newly independent neighboring states. And in anticipation of an Algerian settlement, France wanted to retain control of this oil and mineral rich "part" of Algeria or, failing that, to supervise its exploitation in conjunction with several of her former colonies bordering on the Desert. This French strategy naturally made for quarrels among the African states themselves.

However, whether the Community should disappear or become meaningless, France's permanent contribution to the new Africa will turn out to have been not at all political, like Britain's, but cultural, especially in the fine arts, including literature and cuisine. In searching for suitable political procedures, few Africans will turn to the France that had engaged in the *mission civilisatrice*. But in writing about this effort and in eulogizing the success with which it may be crowned, many Africans will employ what continues to be the language of civilization and culture par excellence, as did *La Liberté*, the newspaper of the *Parti Démocratique de Guinée*, when it spoke of

> union, a word like friendship, goodness, an abstract thing having no face, raising no concrete image in the mind. It goes into all sauces; it accommodates itself to irreconcilables.[9]

[9] *La Liberté*, November 23, 1954, quoted by Ruth Schachter, *ibid.*, p. 307.

Chapter X

Ghana and Nigeria:
The Political Kingdom Gained

The suggestion that there is, or can be in the visible future, such a thing as a "West African Nation" is as manifest an absurdity as that there is, or can be, an "European Nation," at all events until the arrival of the Millennium.[1]

> —Sir Hugh Clifford, Governor of Nigeria (1920)

I will publicly admit that I have never claimed to be a New Messiah, although for reasons best known to a section of the West African Press I have been elevated to that creditable and immortal position. It is possible that I may be one of the apostles of the new Africa.[2]

> —Dr. Azikiwe (1950, a decade before he became Governor-General of Nigeria)

Nation-Building or "Political Institutional Transfer"?

Ghana was the first colony in Black Africa to gain independence, in 1957. Nigeria, in 1960, was the most populous. In both, the transition from British administration to full independence and membership in the Commonwealth took place smoothly, with a minimum of violence. The stages of constitutional advancement through which the two territories passed were roughly parallel to each other and to those passed

[1] Quoted by James S. Coleman, *Nigeria: Background to Nationalism*, p. 193.
[2] Nnamdi Azikiwe, *Renascent Africa*, p. 17, quoted by Coleman, *op. cit.*, p. 302.

through on the road from dependence to independence by other British colonies, ever since Canada set the pattern after the United States had broken away. But the parallelism was only a rough one, because the problems faced by the two territories and their administrators were not identical. African participation in politics and responsibility for government was expanded in a series of constitutional conferences, held at irregular intervals, convened by the British Government whenever local dissatisfaction with the incumbent constitution had built up so much steam that expansion of the constitutional kettle seemed the best way of preventing an explosion. All along the process, beginning late in the nineteenth century, the broad outlines of each successive model were known in advance, because of previous experience in older colonies: establishment of the governor's executive council and of a nominated legislative council; appointment of some Africans to the latter council; indirect and then direct election of the "unofficial" council minority; appointment of Africans to the executive council; an unofficial majority in legislative council and designation of its African head as leader of government business, then as chief minister, and finally as prime minister; gradual removal of official members of council, until full parliamentary-cabinet government on the Westminster model has been reached, and the governor or governor-general plays the symbolic, nonpolitical role of constitutional monarch as personal representative of the British Queen.

This foreknowledge of their general road toward self-government undoubtedly helped to convert potential violence into (occasionally over-dramatized) exercises of a bargaining process, whose fundamental rules were well known to all participants. Especially in West Africa the only serious issue between independence movements and Great Britain was the pace of advancement, not its goal or the road by which to reach it, at least since World War II. Both British and Africans could, therefore, afford to make extremist threats to each other and generally to exaggerate their position, even if this meant periodic imprisonment for the Africans. For example, the President of the Zikist Movement—composed of the more militant followers of Dr. Azikiwe's National Council of Nigeria and the Cameroons (NCNC)—said in 1949:

> I hate the Union Jack with all my heart because it divides the people wherever it goes. . . . It is a symbol of persecution, of domination, a symbol of exploitation, . . . [of] brutality.[3]

Dr. Azikiwe and Dr. Nkrumah delivered themselves of many similar statements. Each alleged at one time that he was the intended victim

[3] *Ibid.*, p. 298.

of an assassination plot, apparently with British connivance. Each was
denounced by British officials as an extremist; e.g., Dr. Nkrumah as
"imbued with a Communist ideology which only political expediency
had blurred," who had "never abandoned his aims for a Union of West
African Soviet Socialist Republics. . . ." [4] And each, after his country
achieved independence, kept on the best of terms with Great Britain.
President Nkrumah accepted appointment to Her Majesty's Privy Council and, more important, kept Ghana in the Commonwealth. And
"Zik," previously referred to as a "nationalist firebrand," as the first
Nigerian Governor-General of the Federation of Nigeria, became Her
Majesty's personal representative in his country.

Here again we have to be careful not to misunderstand African
leaders by imputing conventional meanings to conventional words they
use. Even in North America and Continental Europe, the same words
(in different languages), like *state, nation, official,* have different meanings and impacts. Such differences are bound to be much greater between
the Africans and ourselves, in view of their new and unique political
problems. We must beware also of distorting African realities by studying them only in terms of our conventional tools of analysis, even
though familiarity may make this most convenient for us. In one respect,
we have been violating the last caution in this book, by treating Africa
"south of the Sahara" as an "area" for separate study. Pan-Africanists
have denounced any such compartmentalization of their Continent, into
Africa south and north of the Sahara, Black and White Africa, Tropical
Africa, and so forth, as a manifestation of "neo-colonialism." This
criticism is valid at least to the extent that the Sahara Desert has served
as a communications link more than a barrier, across which caravans have
carried people, goods, and ideas, like ships across the ocean. One should
not criticize the focus of individual "country studies," like the pioneering
ones by Professor Apter of Ghana and by Professor Coleman of Nigeria,
particularly because both show the (British) West African—as distinguished from the Ghanaian or Nigerian—origins and relations of these
two movements to independence. The availability of such studies of individual territories has led students of African politics to engage in the
kind of compare-and-contrast exercises, with which students of comparative government elsewhere are familiar. In the 1960's, it still makes sense
to contrast two states, because they achieved independence three and a
half years apart from one another, but even in the "visible future" this
period is likely to be regarded as but a grain in the sands of time, especially in Africa where so much "history" is being telescoped into so
little time.

The Gold Coast was deliberately selected by the British Government

[4] Watson Commission (1948), quoted by David E. Apter, *op. cit.,* pp. 169f.

as a pilot training project in advancement toward self-government.[5] The foreshortening of the initial timetable of twenty-five to a mere ten years shows how rapidly the "visibility" into the future was improving in West Africa. Nigeria could have had its independence at the same time, as far as the British were concerned, since they wanted to unburden themselves of this responsibility as much as of Uganda, but felt compelled to delay for similar reasons. Nigeria is culturally very diverse. The diversity is especially apparent in differences between the Northern Region, with its Muslim culture, dominated by the Hausa—whose emirates led Lugard to introduce Indirect Rule—but populated by people about 60 per cent of whom are not Hausa speaking; the Western Region, where the urbanized Yorubas are dominant; and the Eastern Region, where the Ibos who predominate were considered not to have any true political systems at all. Because British control originally extended to Lagos, now the federal capital, alone and the first all-Nigerian Legislative Council including representatives of the Northern Region was not set up until 1947, this relatively backward area and its conservative "natural rulers" amounted to a decelerating factor in the independence equation. The solution found under British prodding was a federal system consisting of three Regions, which are equally represented in the Nigerian Senate, while the Northern Region has the strongest representation in the House of Representatives, since it is the most heavily populated. The three major parties began and continued mainly as regional parties. As a result, the House of Representatives with which the Federation passed into independence was composed as follows: Northern People's Congress—150; NCNC (mainly Eastern Region and Ibo)—88; Action Group (mainly Western Region and Yoruba)—74. NPC and NCNC formed a coalition under the prime ministership of Sir Abubakar Tafawa Balewa of the NPC. Dr. Azikiwe, who had been Premier of the Eastern Region, assumed the Presidency of the Senate before becoming Governor-General. Chief Obafemi Awolowo, leader of the Action Group, who had been Premier of the Western Region, became Leader of the Opposition in the Federal House. Of the three regional Premiers, only the Sardauna of Sokoto, leader of the NPC, resisted the trend to move to the federal center of politics and government.

All this looked very much like the kind of nation-building through federalism that had succeeded to varying degrees in other culturally diverse former British colonies, like Canada and India. Hence Professor Coleman's book "is primarily concerned with the processes of nation-building and national awakening in Nigeria." [6] Though on a much

---

[5] See page 18, above.
[6] *Ibid.*, p. 423.

smaller scale, Ghana faced similar problems of diversity. Again the coastal region, i.e., the Gold Coast, was first to come under regular British control, with nominated executive and legislative councils being set up in 1850. The first African member of the legislative council was appointed in 1888. But the Ashanti Federation who occupied the next belt of territory inland were finally defeated by the British only in 1901, Ashanti was not represented in Legco until 1946, and the relatively backward Northern Territories were left out even then. Because they were dealing with a population of less than 5,000,000—more than half of it in the old Gold Coast Colony—and for other reasons, the British overruled local advocates of federalism, and quasi-federalist regional councils were abolished soon after independence, though their position had apparently been "entrenched" in the independence Constitution. Because ethnic diversity was less of a problem in Ghana than in Nigeria, and because the Gold Coast was first to make the transition from British colony to independent member of the Commonwealth, it has been examined as a case study of the transfer of "British-type structures." The "central theme" of Professor Apter's *The Gold Coast in Transition* is, therefore, "political institutional transfer." [7]

The Beginnings of African Innovation

Writing in 1955, Professor Apter suggested three major sources from which political institutions could be transferred: the traditional system of tribe, lineage, clan, and chief; Marxism, with the Soviet Union as the model; and the British parliamentary pattern.[8] To these, Professor Henry L. Bretton has added another, "A very real source of inspiration, not unknown to students of politics, namely opportunism or expediency."[9] While Apter considered the British pattern the probable victorious source, Bretton singled out the "totalitarian orientation" of the Convention Peoples Party (CPP), which he compared with "Communist or Fascist parties, making allowance for organizational deficiencies."[10] Neither of these political scientists seriously considered the possibility of either the transformation of those foreign institutions, parliamentary or totalitarian, that might be transferred, or innovation resulting from adaptation of Ghanaian institutions and procedures. Yet a good deal of transformation and innovation has occurred since

[7] David E. Apter, *op. cit.*, pp. 8f.

[8] *Ibid.*, pp. 17-19.

[9] Henry L. Bretton, "Current Political Thought and Practice in Ghana," *American Political Science Review*, LII, No. 1 (March 1958), p. 50.

[10] *Ibid.*, p. 57.

independence in 1957, especially through adoption of the Constitution of the Republic of Ghana of 1960. Many basic British parliamentary procedures have been retained, though Apter was worried in this respect, because he thought their legitimacy rested mainly upon Dr. Nkrumah's personal charisma. Retention of these important foundations of procedural consensus must be ascribed in large part to the fact that all major politicians had ascended to positions of prominence through (in some cases brief) parliamentary careers, thereby gaining a commitment to the "rules of the game" similar to what we have found in other British territories. The availability of nearly 200 lawyers (Nigeria had nearly 800), most of them trained in Great Britain, also served to strengthen this general procedural commitment. Experience with parliamentary procedures in Ashanti and the Northern Territories had been much shorter, and commitment to the substantive values of traditionalism was stronger there, which perhaps lent some credibility to CPP and Government allegations that its Opposition, in alliance with these conservative groups, was plotting secession, assassination, and civil disorder. The Government used these charges to deport some Opposition leaders and to keep others in "preventive detention." The Opposition was able to campaign in the elections of 1956 and 1960, though considerable electoral intimidation and some violence were reported. In the first Republican Parliament of Ghana, the Opposition amounted to only one-tenth of the membership.

The label of "police state" or "totalitarianism" has been pinned on Ghana on these and similar grounds. Ghana's defenders, on the other hand, have found parallels between these policies and the Alien and Sedition Acts in an equally young United States of America. None of these comparisons seems valid, if we understand correctly the goals pursued by Ghanaian politicians and their perception of the problems they face on the road toward these goals. Such an understanding is hard for us to gain, because even Dr. Nkrumah, and other Africans elsewhere, have admitted that they themselves are still groping their way toward these goals and their expression. Perhaps we can best approach them by stating what these goals are *not*. First of all, the West African leaders do not want to transfer either Western or Soviet political institutions to their countries. This also means that they do not want to make Ghana or Nigeria into nation-states like France or Germany, or West Africa into a Union of West African Soviet Socialist Republics. Their commitment to the creation of larger associations of communities is too strong for the first alternative, their disinclination for organized violence and large-scale discipline seems strong enough to rule out the second.

Moreover, not only words but also actions take on a different meaning in a different environment. For example, African notions of time and space lend a less unpleasant aspect to arrests than they have to us, especially in cases of political detention prior to independence. Dr. Nkrumah himself and most of his lieutenants proudly added the letters "P.G.," for "prison graduate," to their names. Of course, by now, His Excellency Kwame Nkrumah, President and Commander-in-Chief of Ghana, has, as a Privy Councillor, graduated from P.G. to P.C., but political arrests are still likely to appear in different lights to him and his detainees, and, say, Hitler and victims of the Gestapo. Similarly, elections and referenda rarely seem to have the same meaning to Africans that they have in the politically older parts of the globe. The tremendous majorities frequently rolled up by the winning side—as in the French Community referendum, and also in the referendum on Ghana's Republican Constitution[11]—in a whole country on the one hand, or in individual voting districts on the other, suggest that voters are less interested in their opportunity to choose among candidates or programs, than in the very idea of participation in a process which enjoys prestige because it is so novel and modern. "Card-holding membership" in a political party is valued for similar reasons, especially by illiterate people who cannot even read their membership cards. Elections and party membership thus perform functions quite different from those of their apparent models in both constitutional democracies of the West and the Soviet regimes behind the Iron Curtain, where total participation and consent are rigidly enforced; in the Ghana plebiscite just mentioned, only 54 per cent of the eligible voters actually went to the polls.

The Republican Constitution of 1960 and institutional changes accompanying it may suggest some further goals that the builders of the new Africa are not pursuing. For example, the chamber in which Parliament meets was remodelled into the shape of a horseshoe from the "British-type" rectangular arrangement, under which the Government and Opposition front benches face each other to engage in their constant dialectic over clearly defined issues and questions. That the National Assembly[12] was meant to have mainly deliberative functions is also shown by the constitutional position of the President—especially the first President—which endows him with great capacity for independent action. The first President may, according to the last Article of the Constitution, "give directions by legislative instrument," that is, legislate by decree, but he may not amend the Constitution, and he is subject

[11] For—1,008,740, Against—131,425; Nkrumah for President—1,016,076, Danquah for President—124,623, *West Africa*, May 7, 1960, p. 523.

[12] Parliament, according to the Constitution, consists of the President and the National Assembly, just as the British Parliament consists of the Queen and the two Houses.

to the original jurisdiction of the Supreme Court "in all matters where a question arises whether an enactment was made in excess of the powers conferred on Parliament by or under the Constitution. . . ." [13] After the tenure of the first President,

> if contested, an election held by reason of a dissolution of the National Assembly shall be decided by preferences given before the General Election by persons subsequently returned as Members of Parliament, or, if no candidate for election as President obtains more than one-half of the preferences so given, by secret ballot of the Members of the new Parliament;
>
> if contested, an election held by reason of the death or resignation of the President shall be decided by secret ballot of the Members of Parliament.[14]

These provisions were designed to avoid the possibility of Presidency and Legislature being in the hands of opposing parties, as they have often been in the United States. They are of interest also because, through the introductory phrase, "if contested," they anticipate the possibility of unanimity and the absence of a second candidate.

The Constitution also provides for an oath, not unlike that prescribed by the American Constitution for the President of the United States (and used as an argument in the religious controversy of the campaign of 1960 by President Kennedy) which the President takes "before the people" upon assuming office. In addition, he has to make a "solemn declaration before the people" immediately after taking the oath. Among the "fundamental principles" to which he declares his adherence are the following:

> That the union of Africa should be striven for by every lawful means and, when attained, should be faithfully preserved.
>
> That the Independence of Ghana should not be surrendered or diminished on any grounds other than the furtherance of African unity.
>
> That no person should suffer discrimination on grounds of sex, race, tribe, religion or political belief.
>
> That subject to such restrictions as may be necessary for preserving public order, morality or health, no person should be deprived of freedom of religion or speech, of the right to move and assemble without hindrance or of the right of access to courts of law.[15]

Dr. Nkrumah was literally "enstooled" as President, much as chiefs of the Ashanti and other tribes have been enthroned on the stool that

---

[13] *Constitution of the Republic of Ghana*, Articles 55 and 42.
[14] *Ibid.*, Article 11.
[15] *Ibid.*, Article 13.

symbolized the unity of the tribe. Apter suggested that the chieftaincy "represents the orientational base out of which the charismatic authority of Nkrumah . . . developed." [16] He could hardly have foreseen that the new institutions of Ghana would also draw upon another adaptable procedure of tribal society in the old Gold Coast, in the course of political innovation. Apter calls this tribal society

> . . . essentially contractual in the classic sense of the word. The ceremony of contract was repeated at intervals throughout the political life of the tribe, throughout its various administrative levels. The contract could be broken, hence the crucial importance of swearing an oath.[17]

The Ghana Constitution no more than any other can give protection against descent to political perdition or assurance of ascent to Dr. Nkrumah's political Kingdom of Heaven. It can show outsiders the rather special content hell and heaven have for Africans in the post-independence era. Hell would seem to consist of loss of their newly gained independence to anyone, not only their former rulers who, in any case, are not desirous of reassuming their old burden. Heaven, as most Utopias, consists of many vague things—more than are contained in the (by contrast) almost ascetic sounding goals stated in the Preamble to the Constitution of the United States. Above all, it includes the independence and then the unity of all of Africa.

Western critics have denounced the Nkrumah Constitution as both the foundation of and façade for a police state (and some communist critics, uninterested in constitutions, have denounced Nkrumah as a representative of the "national bourgeoisie"). The critical position of the West is weak, however, because almost every democratic constitution designed in the twentieth century has materially contributed to the failure to provide that dynamic equilibrium of stability and flexibility, acceptability and efficiency, which is the hallmark of political success.[18] Recent history is littered with the wreckage of constitutions declaring citizens' rights, designed by the best available talent in political science, jurisprudence, sociology, and philosophy. Nor do Westerners, when they preach their values, like individualism, private property, or competition, speak from a position of moral strength to Africans—especially to Africans living on the Gold Coast, between the Ivory Coast and what used to be known as the Slave Coast (of Nigeria). Even advocacy of Christian values often seems hypocritical, particularly in areas with white

[16] Apter, *op. cit.*, p. 108.
[17] *Ibid.*, pp. 116f.
[18] See Herbert J. Spiro, *Government by Constitution: The Political Systems of Democracy*, chapter 25, "New Political Systems," and *passim*.

settlers. Although many missionaries were highly respected and are fondly remembered, there are always stories about the Reverend So-and-So, "who came with the Bible in his hands and owning nothing but the shirt on his back—and now we have the Bible and he has 10,000 acres."

We are not here taking a relativist position. We are not saying that all values are relative to their "cultural context" and that, therefore, it makes no sense to criticize Ghanaian values, and the Constitution that symbolizes and is meant to bolster them, by American standards. There are certain rockbottom values that come close to having universal validity for mankind, because they come out of the universals of the human condition. It is the task of the politicians of any system to articulate these values, ideals, or goals in understandable terms, by pointing to those problems which in their particular situation are the greatest obstacles on the road toward fulfillment, and then giving leadership in their removal. And it is the difficult task of constitution-builders to find procedures for the handling of problems, procedures that will remain fundamentally stable over time, though they must be flexible enough to adjust to changes in the environment; procedures that can produce efficient solutions to the problems the people consider most important; procedures that, above all, are themselves acceptable to the people. Many modern constitutions have failed because they did not address themselves to the most pressing problems of their time, and because they failed to avail themselves of procedures familiar to those people whose participation the constitution called for. This latter failure was not always the fault of the constitution builders, because frequently they had no indigenous procedural raw material to work with, and because the people's inexperience made them incapable of cooperative communal action.[19] No such handicap exists in Ghana or elsewhere in sub-Saharan Africa. The authors of the Republican Constitution of Ghana deserve some credit for seeking to capitalize upon their people's procedural know-how, as they elicit consensus for new goals by embodying these in the fundamental charter of their new political system. No one will quarrel with the goals stated in the Preamble:

WE THE PEOPLE OF GHANA, by our Representatives gathered in this our Constituent Assembly,

IN EXERCISE of our undoubted right to appoint for ourselves the means whereby we shall be governed,

IN SYMPATHY with and loyalty to our fellow-countrymen of Africa,

[19] E.g., see Edward C. Banfield, *The Moral Basis of a Backward Society*, which describes a procedurally underdeveloped Italian village.

IN THE HOPE that we may by our actions this day help to further the development of a Union of African States, and

IN A SPIRIT of friendship and peace with all other peoples of the World,

DO HEREBY ENACT and give to ourselves this Constitution.

This Constitution seems more likely to succeed than would one whose institutions and procedures had been transplanted to Ghana from a different soil and climate.

West African Federalism

Nigeria, like Ghana, was launched into independence by Great Britain with British institutions and procedures, but unlike Ghana, it was given a federal system. Federalism was the solution to the problem posed by the traditionalism of the Muslim emirates of the North, which had stayed stable under the umbrella of Indirect Rule. It was his encounter with these firmly established political systems that led Sir Frederick Lugard to formulate the theory of Indirect Rule in the first place. The emirates had been remnants of an empire founded in a Muslim holy war at the beginning of the nineteenth century. Islam itself had been dominant in Northern Nigeria since the fifteenth century. One feature especially distinguished the emirates, their regular systems of taxation. This enabled the British colonial administration to use them as administrative arms, while permitting them to retain their own traditional customs, laws, and rulers, always subject to British interference. Leaders of independence movements were later to criticize Indirect Rule as one gambit in the British "imperialist" game played according to the motto, "divide and conquer." Small units of administration were perpetuated by Indirect Rule, local government was left in the hands of traditionalist "natural rulers," and "the task of welding diverse elements into a Nigerian nation" was complicated.[20] Professor Coleman, writing in 1958, found "The contrast with neighboring French territories . . . quite striking." Although interterritorial parties like the *Rassemblement Démocratique Africain* had been permitted and even encouraged by the French administration, French West Africa was to break up into its seven component parts two years later. Nigeria actually achieved independence as one Federation, even though its population was about double that of all French West Africa.

Maintenance of the unity of Nigeria during the transition from colonial administration to independence was no easy matter, and the survival of the Federation of Nigeria as the most populous African political

---

[20] Coleman, *op. cit.*, p. 53.

system still appears doubtful to many. The chief threats came from the extreme cultural diversity of the "country" and the related differences in political development, especially between the south and north. As one result of this, the Western and Eastern Regions were granted self-government in 1957, more than two years before the political leaders of the Northern Region (the "natural rulers") considered their area ready for it. Chief Awolowo, a barrister and leader of the Yoruba-based Action Group, became Premier of the Western Region. Dr. Azikiwe, leader of the Ibo-based NCNC, became Premier of the Eastern Region, having just won an increased majority in its House of Assembly, although a special Commission of Enquiry had just criticized him for improper conduct by permitting investment of public moneys in an African bank in which he had a personal interest.

While the two southern regions gained self-government, a Federal Cabinet was set up, led by the first Nigerian Prime Minister, Alhaji Abubakar Tafawa Balewa of the Northern Peoples' Congress. The NPC, however, continues to be led by the Premier of the Northern Region, Alhaji Ahmadu, Sardauna of Sokoto. In what may by now strike us as a "typically African" move, the Prime Minister invited both NCNC and Action Group to join him in a "national" coalition and succeeded in forming an all-party government. This was short-lived, since the Action Group soon found itself opposing an NPC-NCNC coalition. Politics at the federal level was conducted along the British pattern: Government *versus* Opposition. A period of intense constitutional bargaining between the parties, and between Nigerians and the British, followed, involving repeated threats to the unity of the incipient Federation. The solution to the problem of unity was found in an elaborate and complicated federal constitution that included a lengthy Bill of Rights. The Nigerian Federal Constitution was a lawyers' document, entirely in the tradition of the English Common Law with its procedural orientation. This was demonstrated by a "seminar" on the new Constitution, held a few months before Independence Day, in which Nigerian judges and lawyers were advised on the problems of federal constitutionalism by distinguished jurists from the Commonwealth and the United States. In some respects, this background of independence may have contributed to stabilizing the Federation. Because of the longer preparation, the slower phasing of constitutional advancement, and the stronger substantive internal disagreements than those faced by Ghana or the French colonies, negotiations in Nigeria, conducted with British procedures and under British supervision, were protracted; the main issues were difficult to resolve; and much compromise was required. Nigerian politicians therefore acquired a maximum of experience with these procedures and may have acquired very strong commitment to them. Often, the greater the effort required to achieve certain goals, the more highly are they valued, once gained.

We have already noticed one sign pointing in this direction, the transfer of the Eastern and Western Regional Premiers, Dr. Azikiwe as Governor-General and Chief Awolowo as Leader of the Opposition to the federal center. While the real leaders of the Northern Region resisted this centripetal trend, their representatives in the Federal Government, including the Prime Minister, showed great independence from regional ties on sensitive questions of federal policy; for example, when the Muslim Federal Prime Minister resisted Northern Muslim pressure against signing a trade agreement with Israel. However, during the first year of independence there were also counter-indications suggesting that the constitutional compromise might not endure for long. For example, the Government of the Northern Region increased the number of seats in its House of Assembly in order to reduce the proportional strength of the Action Group, which had been strong in certain constituencies. The federal NPC-NCNC coalition also passed, by the requisite amending majorities of two-thirds of both Federal Houses, a bill to establish a fourth "Mid-West" state, to be carved out of the Opposition-dominated Western Region.

The issue of territorial organization had long agitated Nigerian independence movements, whose leaders frequently changed their stands as they detected advantageous or deleterious effects upon their own political fortunes in one or another arrangement. For instance, in 1950, Dr. Azikiwe asserted that the tripartite regionalism of Nigeria was "an artificial creation and must inevitably tend towards Balkanization." [21] At other times, he favored a federal Nigeria of eight units, a unitary state, or, again in 1950, ten "main ethnic and/or linguistic groups." In trying to understand these changes of mind we should always remember their West African setting. Sir Hugh Clifford, in the statement at the beginning of this chapter, ridiculed the idea of a "West African Nation," not of a Nigerian nation, which might have seemed even more laughable to him. For eight years, soon after Lagos became a British colony, it was administered by the Governor of the West African Settlements, stationed in Sierra Leone (which got its independence within a year of Nigeria). For another twelve years, until 1886, Lagos Colony came under the Governor of the Gold Coast. When Dr. Azikiwe returned "home" from attending American colleges and universities, he launched a political newspaper, the *West African Pilot,* not in Lagos, but in Accra, capital of the Gold Coast. Similarly, the early contacts and influence of American Negro advocates of Pan-Africanism, like Dr. W. E. B. Du Bois, Marcus Garvey, and George Padmore, were with West Africans, as the most

[21] Quoted by Coleman, *op. cit.,* p. 348.

advanced Africans of the time, not with men whom they thought of, or who thought of themselves as Nigerians, Gold Coasters, Senegalese, or Liberians. In other words, in West as in East Africa, the problems of territorial organization created by cultural diversity seem as difficult as they do, because they are being defined in terms of European categories. If, on the other hand, the West Africans look at their situation in the light of their own widely held goal of the creation of more encompassing associations of African communities, then half their present problems may evaporate, and the remainder may be more easily solved through innovation and adaptation.

The End of Tradition?

However, one major difference between West and East Africa will seriously handicap efforts to innovate and to adapt old local procedures to West Africa's modernizing needs: the existence of traditional Islamic political systems. They share none of the unique political traits of the new African states and of their leadership. They were established through the use of organized force, often in holy wars. Even though located on the rim of the Sahara Desert, their well organized administrative systems were defined by fairly clear notions of territoriality that were, moreover, reënforced through the superimposition of European rule. Literacy in the Arabic alphabet, though confined to the political and religious elite, facilitated historical consciousness and Muslim cultural differentiation. For the relatively undifferentiated judicial process of the peoples whom they conquered, Muslim rulers substituted kadi-administered Koranic law.[22] As heirs to Aristotelian logic, and as operators of a clearly defined power structure, the Muslims recognize the irreconcilability of mutually exclusive opposites as much as anyone brought up in the European tradition. As communicants of a religion requiring observance of a rigid calendar and punctuality at daily and weekly prayers, and as participants in a culture that made great contributions to the development of algebra (an Arabic word), the Muslim ruling classes have not been existing in a continuum of timelessness or numberlessness. Ever since the founding of Muslim kingdoms like the original Ghana—in the present-day territory of the Republic of Mali (the name of another such kingdom)—in the European Middle Ages, their faithful maintained religious and commercial contacts with the rest of the Arab world in North Africa and the Near East. Today Islam is the fastest spreading religion south of the Sahara.

That Islamic political theory is highly adaptable is shown by the

[22] See J. Spencer Trimmingham, *Islam in West Africa*, chapter 6 and *passim*.

diverse directions in which leaders like President Bourguiba of Tunisia, President Nasser of the United Arab Republic, President Kassim of Iraq, President Ayub Khan of Pakistan, and King Ibn Saud of Saudi Arabia have taken their respective countries. The British policy of Indirect Rule in Northern Nigeria discouraged political modernization in general and popular participation in particular until just before the unwelcome arrival of independence. At that point, the traditional elite was still able to mobilize the newly enfranchised population in support of the conservative NPC. This left the problems of self-modernization and broadening to this elite, upon which the lower strata, partly under southern influences, would be making increasing demands. The NPC's numerically superior position in the Federal Parliament and Government will help it meet some of these demands, but in case of failure to do so adequately, the resultant conflict in Northern Nigeria might well take on conventional Muslim rather than unconventional African characteristics. The effects of such a revolution on the Federation of Nigeria, as well as on the course of political innovation in all of Africa south of the Sahara, could be disastrous.

In the south of Africa, the peculiarly isolationist Christianity of the Afrikaners had created the greatest threat to the emergence of a healthy new politics. In the north of the Continent, the greatest obstacle was posed by the artificially induced longevity of emirates that were remnants of a holy war conducted by a great Muslim empire builder more than a century and a half ago. Former French territories whose populations contained a proportion of Muslims as high as or higher than Northern Nigeria, like Senegal or Guinea, did not face the same problem, because the French had not practiced Indirect Rule.[23] This made it easier for the new Ghana to experiment with Guinea and the new Mali in working out new forms of association, than for the new Federation of Nigeria to resume and strengthen its old British West African contacts. All over sub-Saharan Africa, the primitive, the ancient, the medieval, the modern, the contemporary, and futuristic were being blended by unprecedented methods. In consequence, both Governor Clifford and his successor, Dr. Azikiwe, were proved right—the latter as an apostle of the new Africa and the former, because neither the Millennium nor a West African Nation has arrived. But something greater *is* arriving, something whose outlines are but dimly perceived even by its creators.

[23] The percentages of Muslims were as follows: Northern Nigeria 69, Ghana 6.5, Guinea 65, Senegal (with Mauretania) 78, Niger 85. From Trimmingham, *op. cit.*, p. 333.

Chapter XI

The Future

> *They refused to understand the role that, on a day not far off,
> the African continent will play in the new equilibrium of a world
> in transformation, when the people, all the people, will have
> occupied their sovereign place in the United Nations. . . .*
> *The African continent represents a question mark. May our
> message and that of all the honest people of the world contribute
> to find the just response to the question which Africa addresses to
> you about its destiny.*[1]
>
> —Sékou Touré

The End of Colonialism: The Portuguese Case

That colonialism will have ended in Africa south of the Sahara
about two decades after the founding of the United Nations seems
virtually certain. "However, African history in our days is undergoing
such an acceleration that decisive and important events punctuate the
process at an unexpected rhythm."[2] Until 1961, most of the punctuation
consisted of commas, colons, and periods. The exclamation marks, bullets,
were rarely used before the uprising in Portuguese Angola. Angola and
Mozambique were the two largest and most populous territories still
under European rule. Nevertheless, under the combined pressures of
African uprisings and Allied dissent, Portugal was losing the total
commitment to her control that constitutes the only effective resistance
against contemporary African independence movements. Less than half
a year after the first Angolan killings, Premier Salazar's Government

---

[1] "Africa's Destiny," in *Africa Speaks,* James Duffy and Robert A. Manners, eds.,
pp. 35 and 47.
[2] *Ibid.,* p. 35.

offered Africans "constitutional equality." Even before the uprising,
Captain Galvao's dramatic seizure of the Portuguese liner "Santa Maria"
demonstrated the existence of an internal opposition to Dr. Salazar's
regime, led by a distinguished former colonial administrator, for whom
reforms in Africa were a very important African goal. Portugal discovered
that it could afford a costly colonial war even less than France, whose
closer Algerian conflict was in its seventh year. Portugal's allies in NATO
even let the British Foreign Secretary, Lord Home, tell a gathering of
Portuguese notables in Lisbon, in public, that the United Kingdom
had always found it useful to set a time table of colonial constitutional
advancement. The Anglo-Portuguese alliance is regarded as the oldest surviving alliance between two states in the world, and Lord Home was
listened to with some respect, even while United States votes against Portugal at the United Nations were denounced as currying favor with the
Africans to gain their support against the communists. These fulmi-
nations could be regarded as requests for American economic aid to Portugal in exchange for a less repressive African policy on her part. They
also suggested that loss of her African possessions would have much more
disastrous repercussions upon Portuguese domestic politics, than did
loss of the Congo upon Belgium.

The Old and the New

While colonialism was coming to its end, the two oldest sub-Saharan
sovereignties were trying to adjust to the new Africa that was growing
up all around them. Both Ethiopia and Liberia sponsored conferences
of continental scope in their capitals. The rulers of both visited the
heads of various newly independent African states. Both countries
mounted modernization programs, Liberia with American help, Ethiopia
with the assistance of a finely balanced assortment of foreigners, including both Americans and Russians. Both identified themselves with
the general African opposition to South Africa by jointly bringing suit
against it before the International Court on the issue of its administration
of South-West Africa. Ethiopia and Liberia brought this suit, because
they had been the only African members of the League of Nations,
whose mandate the Union of South Africa was to execute in the former
German colony. Ethiopia seemed to be having a harder time than Liberia
in achieving equal partnership with the new states, because its Emperor
was so much more obviously an autocratic ruler than Liberia's five-term
President Tubman. Emperor Haile Selassie was able to suppress a
"palace revolt" against himself with considerable loss of life. Since he
spends a higher proportion of national income for military purposes

than any other sub-Saharan state, he could also be expected to defend Ethiopian territory in disputes with Somalis, for whom the new Republic of Somali spoke up after gaining statehood in 1960. But it seemed unlikely that his "old regime" would survive himself if, indeed, it would last that long.

Whatever happens to these two oldest of African states, history in the new ones will continue to accelerate, having started at the zero point. The question behind President Sékou Touré's "question mark" is whether the speed ultimately attained will fit the new Africa into the dynamic "new equilibrium of a world in transformation." Once all Africa south of the Sahara Desert and north of the Limpopo River has gained its independence, *it* will no longer address a question about its destiny to *us*, because it will be fully responsible for shaping its own destiny. The goal of independence will no longer present problems, since it will have been achieved and have been replaced by new goals. Modernization will be among the most important of these, but it will be overshadowed by movements for Pan-African unions for as long, at least, as the Republic of South Africa continues on the tragic, self-destructive path on which it was launched in 1948. Africans north of the Limpopo will cooperate in order to help Africans south of the River. African states at the United Nations will use the leverage that the Cold War gives them in order to apply maximum pressure to the Republic of South Africa, and in this sense Premier Salazar's criticism of United States African policy was not beside the point. The parties to the Cold War will continue to curry favor with their formal equals from Africa in the world organization, and the tone of world politics will be affected by this phenomenon. This was already true of the debate over Berlin in 1961, when Chancellor Adenauer and his American allies advocated "self-determination" for the people of Berlin, and of East Germany, in hopes that this would strike a responsive note with the newly self-determined Africans. At times, Dr. Adenauer seemed to suggest that the Germans were entitled to self-determination in free elections, *because* "every people in Africa," as he put it, was being accorded this right. This claim overlooked the fact that no people in sub-Saharan Africa had, in the present century, attempted to achieve its goals through the use of military force, and that none was likely to do so in the "visible future." Neither the Germans, nor any other participant in the Cold War, could claim such a happy record.

The Vice of Imitation

Of course, this record was not "earned," and it need not remain so happy as it has been. It was not earned, because the colonial powers did not permit their subject peoples to organize and exercise force, and because the colonial powers withdrew before the occurrence of massive violence. The new African states are relatively disinterested in questions of territorial integrity, not because of moral superiority on their part, but because the frontiers were drawn by the colonial administrations, and because a boundary is a non-African concept. The absence of drives to create cultural homogeneity within the new states, and cultural differentiation between them, must also be attributed, not to African initiative, but to historical accident.

The record need not remain so happy, because some African leaders will want to imitate even the negative aspects of conventional sovereign nation-states as a result of their desire to modernize. Such efforts to emulate the already obsolescent in non-African political institutions will be stimulated especially by unsympathetic outside criticism of African attempts to experiment and to innovate. If Africans heed this kind of criticism—of failure to introduce a two-party system, to foster a middle class, or to follow an anti-inflationary policy, and the like—the dangerous psychological aspects of the "colonial situation" might persist, even though all the colonies gain independence. The former colonial and other white powers would simply transfer their attitude of superiority, and the former colonies theirs of dependence, from Africa to world politics. In other words, "political institutional transfer," while failing itself, would only succeed in transferring pathological psychological attitudes into world politics, whose atmosphere is already contaminated enough. Therefore, it is important that non-Africans exercise restraint in their criticism of or advice to leaders of the new states.

This applies as much to economic and cultural development as to constitutional change. For example, the problems of constructing the educational system of a country, 90 per cent of whose people are illiterate in 1960, are quite different from those of building a school system for American states in the nineteenth century. One important function of literacy in industrial economies revolves around job instructions, e.g., for tractor or lathe operators. But in the age of increasingly less expensive television and otherwise constantly improving communications, a people might conceivably "skip" the phase of mass literacy for some years and still industrialize. Similarly, neither a railway nor a road network may be best designed to suit the development needs of every new African economy. For some mineral and agricultural products, in certain climates, air transport may turn out to be more economical and, again, opportunities may arise to skip stages in industrial development that more mature systems had to pass through, simply because they had neither the experience nor the advice of earlier modernizers to call upon. In the economic field, the Africans should perhaps consider themselves lucky that advice is being offered to them from at least two competing sources, the parties to the Cold War. This widens their choice and is likely to stimulate both their advisers and themselves, at the same time reducing elements of condescension (remnants of the colonial situation) in the outsiders' approach.

Both for economic and cultural development, and for the political and constitutional growth of the new Africa, one thing is needed above all: imaginative and inventive creativity. It is required of all concerned, politicians and diplomats, businessmen and public servants, journalists and scholars, Africans and others. Without imagination and inventiveness, the prophets of Africa's doom may yet be proved right, but their prophecy will have been self-fulfilling. The road signs we have seen in Africa so far point away from disaster and toward success, but they are signs written in a language of the future whose interpreters are yet to be trained, and whose syntax is not yet fully understood, because it is still being formed. The task of understanding is urgent, for, as the Secretary General of the United Nations put it, before he laid down his life in the service of Africa and the world organization:

We are at a turn of the road where our attitude will be of decisive significance . . . not only for the future of [the United Nations] but also for the future of Africa. And Africa may well in present circumstances mean the world.

Statistical Tables

Table I

Population

	Population 000	Density/km²	European 000	Asian 000	Coloured or Other 000
Southern Africa					
Republic of South Africa	14,673	12	2,907	421	1,281
Basutoland	674	22	2		
Bechuanaland	337	0	2.5		
Swaziland	250	14	4		
South West Africa	554	1	62		
Central Africa					
Southern Rhodesia	3,000	8	178		13
Northern Rhodesia	2,360	3	66	7	
Nyasaland	2,770	24	7	10	
Congo (Leopoldville)	13,821	6	102	11	
Ruanda-Urundi	4,780	88	6		
East Africa					
Ethiopia	21,800	18			
Kenya	6,450	11	58	185	5
Mozambique	6,310	8	66	17	35
Somalia	1,990	3			
Tanganyika	9,076	10	28	93	6
Uganda	6,517	27	12	76	
Zanzibar and Pemba	304	115			
West Africa					
Angola	4,550	4	110		30
Cameroun	3,225	7	16		
Gabon	420	2 ⎫			
Congo (Brazzaville)	795	2 ⎪			
Central African Republic	1,185	2 ⎬ 24			1
Chad	2,600	2 ⎭			
Spanish Guinea	216	8			
Portuguese Guinea	565	16			

	Population 000	Density/km²	European 000	Asian 000	Coloured or Other 000
Gambia	301	29			
Ghana	4,911	21	7		
Nigeria	33,663	38	10		
Cameroons, British adm.	1,621	18			
Sierra Leóne	2,400	33			
Liberia	1,125	11			
Dahomey	2,000	17 ⎫			
Guinea	2,727	11			
Ivory Coast	3,103	10			
Mali	4,300	4 ⎬ 88			
Mauritania	730	1			
Niger	2,555	2			
Senegal	2,550	13			
Upper Volta	3,537	13 ⎭			
Togo	1,442	25			
Tropical and Southern Africa	159,000	8			
[United States of America]	177,700	19			

SOURCE: United Nations, Department of Economic and Social Affairs, Statistical Office, *United Nations Demographic Yearbook 1960*. Ethnic statistics, unless cited in the text, are from Department of Economic and Social Affairs, 1959, Table 1-I, "Population by Country and Ethnic Composition, 1956," *Economic Survey of Africa since 1950*.

Table II

Per Capita National Income
of Selected Countries[1]

(in Dollars)

1956 or 1957

Rhodesia and Nyasaland	132
Belgian Congo	76
Kenya	78
Tanganyika	48
Uganda	57
French Equatorial Africa	126
French West Africa	133
Ghana	194
Nigeria	69

Table III

Annual Per Capita Personal Income,
African and Non-African,
in Selected Countries[2]

(in Dollars)

	Belgian Congo	Federation of Rhodesia & Nyasaland	Kenya
Africans			
Money Income	(31.48)	(33.60)	(19.60)
Total Income	43.14	39.20	33.60
Europeans and Other Non-Africans	2,973.46	1,710.80	1,050.40

[1] United Nations, Department of Economic and Social Affairs, *Economic Survey of Africa since 1950*, Table 1-III, p. 15.

[2] *Ibid.*, Table 1-LIV, p. 94.

Selected Bibliography

Chapter I
The New Africa in World Politics

Gunther, John. *Inside Africa*. New York: Harper & Brothers, 1955.

Hailey, Lord. *An African Survey—Revised 1956: A Study of Problems Arising in Africa South of the Sahara*. New York: Oxford University Press, 1957.

Hodgkin, Thomas. *Nationalism in Colonial Africa*. New York: New York University Press, 1957.

Horrabin, J. F. *An Atlas of Africa*. New York: Frederick A. Praeger, 1960.

Kimble, George H. T. *Tropical Africa*. New York: Twentieth Century Fund, 1960. 2 volumes.

Segal, Ronald, ed. *Political Africa: A Who's Who of Personalities and Parties*. New York: Frederick A. Praeger, 1961.

Chapter II
The United Nations and Africa

Bloomfield, Lincoln P. *The United Nations and U.S. Foreign Policy: A New Look at the National Interest*. Boston: Little, Brown and Company, 1960.

Duffy, James, and Robert A. Manners, eds. *Africa Speaks*. New York: D. Van Nostrand Co., 1961.

Emerson, Rupert. *From Empire to Nation: The Rise to Self-Assertion of Asian and African Peoples*. Cambridge, Mass.: Harvard University Press, 1960.

International African Institute (London), *Social Implications of Industrialization and Urbanization in Africa South of the Sahara*. Paris: United Nations Educational, Social and Cultural Organization, 1956.

United Nations, *Yearbook of the United Nations.* New York: Columbia University Press, 1947-.

————, Non-Self-Governing Territories, *Summaries and analyses of information transmitted to the Secretary General during 1946-.* New York: United Nations, 1947-.

————, *Progress of the Non-Self-Governing Territories under the Charter, Territorial Surveys* (vol. 5). New York: United Nations, 1960.

————, Department of Economic and Social Affairs, *Economic Survey of Africa since 1950.* New York: United Nations, 1959.

————, Department of Economic and Social Affairs, Statistical Office, *United Nations Demographic Yearbook 1948-,* and *United Nations Statistical Yearbook 1948-.* New York: United Nations, 1949-.

Chapter III
The United States and Africa

Africa League, *A New American Policy toward Africa.* New York: Africa League, 1960.

African-American Institute, *Africa Special Report,* since 1961 *Africa Report.* Washington: African-American Institute, 1955-.

American Assembly, *The United States and Africa.* New York: The American Assembly, 1958.

American Society of African Culture, *Africa Seen by American Negroes.* Paris: Présense Africaine, 1958.

Bowles, Chester. *Africa's Challenge to America.* Berkeley: University of California Press, 1957.

Padmore, George. *Pan-Africanism or Communism? The Coming Struggle for Africa.* New York: Roy Publishers, 1955.

Chapter IV
South Africa: The Problem of Race

Brookes, Edgar H., and J. B. Macaulay. *Civil Liberty in South Africa.* New York: Oxford University Press, 1958.

Carter, Gwendolen M. *The Politics of Inequality: South Africa since 1948.* New York: Frederick A. Praeger, 1958.

Cowan, D. V. *The Foundations of Freedom: Law and Government in Southern Africa.* New York, Oxford University Press, 1961.

Keppel-Jones, Arthur. *When Smuts Goes: A History of South Africa from 1952-2010, First Published in 2015.* Pietermaritzburg: Shuter & Shooter, 1947.

Chapter V
The British Protectorates: Tradition and Transition

Ashton, Hugh. *The Basuto*. London: Oxford University Press, 1952.
Government of Basutoland, *Constitutional Handbook*. Maseru: Government of Basutoland, 1960.
Fortes, M. and E. E. Evans-Pritchard, eds. *African Political Systems*. London: Oxford University Press, 1940.

Chapter VI
The Rhodesias and Nyasaland: Partnership and Federation

Davidson, J. W. *The Northern Rhodesian Legislative Council*. London: Faber & Faber, 1947.
Franck, Thomas M. *Race and Nationalism: The Struggle for Power in Rhodesia-Nyasaland*. New York: Fordham University Press, 1960.
Kaunda, Kenneth, and Colin Morris. *Black Government?* Lusaka: United Society for Christian Literature, 1960.
Leys, Colin. *European Politics in Southern Rhodesia*. Oxford: Oxford University Press, 1959.
Mason, Philip. *Birth of a Dilemma: The Conquest and Settlement of Rhodesia*. New York: Oxford University Press, 1959.
———. *Year of Decision: Rhodesia and Nyasaland 1960*. New York: Oxford University Press, 1960.
United Kingdom, Advisory Commission on the Review of the Constitution of Rhodesia and Nyasaland, *Report* (Cmnd. 1148). London: H.M. Stationery Office, 1960.

Chapter VII
East Africa: Tribalism and Violence

Apter, David E. *The Political Kingdom in Uganda: A Study in Bureaucratic Nationalism*. Princeton: Princeton University Press, 1961.
Castagno, A. A. *Somalia*. New York: Columbia University Press, 1959.
Fallers, Lloyd A. *Bantu Bureaucracy*. Cambridge: W. Heffer & Sons, Ltd., no date.
Mannoni, O. *Prospero and Caliban: The Psychology of Colonization*. New York: Frederick A. Praeger, 1956.
Slater, Montagu. *The Trial of Jomo Kenyatta*, 2nd ed., Revised. London: Secker & Warburg, 1959.

Southall, A. W. and P. C. W. Gutkind. *Townsmen in the Making: Kampala and Its Suburbs.* Kampala: East African Institute of Social Research, 1957.

United Kingdom. Kenya Government, *Historical Survey on the Origin and Growth of Mau Mau* (Cmnd. 1030). London: H.M. Stationery Office, 1960.

————, Nyasaland Commission of Inquiry, *Report* (Cmnd. 814). London: H.M. Stationery Office, 1959.

Young, Roland, and Harry A. Fosbrooke. *Smoke in the Hills: Land and Politics among the Luguru of Tanganyika.* Evanston: Northwestern University Press, 1960.

Chapter VIII

The Congo: Temperament and Time

Carter, Gwendolen M. *Independence for Africa.* New York: Frederick A. Praeger, 1960.

Gluckman, Max. *Custom and Conflict in Africa.* Glencoe: The Free Press, 1959.

————. *The Judicial Process among the Barotse of Northern Rhodesia.* Manchester: Manchester University Press, 1955.

Legum, Colin. *Congo Disaster.* Baltimore: Penguin Books, 1961.

Merriam, Alan P. *Congo: Background of Conflict.* Evanston: Northwestern University Press, 1961.

Northrop, F. S. C. *The Meeting of East and West: An Inquiry Concerning World Understanding.* New York: Macmillan Co., 1946.

Chapter IX

French Africa: The Civilizing Mission

Betts, Raymond F. *Assimilation and Association in French Colonial Theory 1890-1914.* New York: Columbia University Press, 1961.

Cowan, L. Gray. *Local Government in West Africa.* New York: Columbia University Press, 1958.

Coleman, James S. *Togoland.* New York: Columbia University Press, 1956.

Hodgkin, Thomas, and Ruth Schachter. *French-Speaking West Africa in Transition.* New York: Columbia University Press, 1961.

Macridis, Roy C., and Bernard E. Brown. *The De Gaulle Republic: The Quest for Unity.* Homewood: Dorsey Press, 1960.

Schachter, Ruth. "Single-Party Systems in West Africa," *American Political Science Review*, Vol. LV, No. 2 (June 1961), pp. 294-307.

Thompson, Virginia, and Richard Adloff. *French West Africa.* Stanford: Stanford University Press, 1958.

————. *The Emerging States of French Equatorial Africa.* Stanford: Stanford University Press, 1960.

Chapter X
Ghana and Nigeria: The Political Kingdom Gained

Apter, David E. *The Gold Coast in Transition.* Princeton: Princeton University Press, 1955.

Banfield, Edward C. *The Moral Basis of a Backward Society.* Glencoe: The Free Press, 1958.

Bretton, Henry L. "Current Political Thought and Practice in Ghana," *American Political Science Review,* Vol. LII, No. 1 (March 1958), pp. 46-63.

Coleman, James S. *Nigeria: Background to Nationalism.* Berkeley: University of California Press, 1958.

Hansard Society, *What are the problems of Parliamentary Government in West Africa?* London: Hansard Society, 1958.

Hodgkin, Thomas. *Nigerian Perspectives: An Historical Anthology.* London: Oxford University Press, 1960.

Mackenzie, W. J. M., and Kenneth Robinson, eds. *Five Elections in Africa.* New York: Oxford University Press, 1960.

Nkrumah, Kwame. *Ghana: The Autobiography of Kwame Nkrumah.* New York: Thomas Nelson & Sons, 1957.

————. *I Speak of Freedom: A Statement of African Ideology.* New York: Frederick A. Praeger, 1961.

Trimmingham, J. Spencer. *Islam in West Africa.* Oxford: Oxford University Press, 1959.

United Kingdom, Commission appointed to enquire into the fears of Minorities and means of allaying them, *Nigeria—Report* (Cmnd. 505). London: H.M. Stationery Office, 1958.

Wight, Martin. *The Gold Coast Legislative Council.* London: Faber & Faber, 1947.

Chapter XI
The Future

Duffy, James. *Portuguese Africa.* Cambridge, Mass.: Harvard University Press, 1959.

Hance, William A. *African Economic Development.* New York: Harper & Brothers, 1958.

Millikan, Max F., and Donald L. M. Blackmer, eds. *The Emerging Nations: Their Growth and United States Policy.* Boston: Little, Brown and Company, 1961.

Index